Practice*Planners*

Arthur E. Jongsma, Jr., Series Editor

Helping therapists help their clients...

Treatment Planners cover all the necessary elements for developing formal treatment plans, including detailed problem definitions, long-term goals, short-term objectives, therapeutic interventions, and DSM-IV™ diagnoses.

☐ The Complete Adult Psychotherapy Treatment Planner, Fourth Edition.................0-471-76346-2 / $49.95
☐ The Child Psychotherapy Treatment Planner, Fourth Edition.............................0-471-78535-0 / $49.95
☐ The Adolescent Psychotherapy Treatment Planner, Fourth Edition ....0-471-78539-3 / $49.95
☐ The Addiction Treatment Planner, Third Edition..0-471-72544-7 / $49.95
☐ The Couples Psychotherapy Treatment Planner ....0-471-24711-1 / $49.95
☐ The Group Therapy Treatment Planner, Second Edition.....................................0-471-66791-9 / $49.95
☐ The Family Therapy Treatment Planner ....0-471-34768-X / $49.95
☐ The Older Adult Psychotherapy Treatment Planner ....0-471-29574-4 / $49.95
☐ The Employee Assistance (EAP) Treatment Planner ....0-471-24709-X / $49.95
☐ The Gay and Lesbian Psychotherapy Treatment Planner ....0-471-35080-X / $49.95
☐ The Crisis Counseling and Traumatic Events Treatment Planner ....0-471-39587-0 / $49.95
☐ The Social Work and Human Services Treatment Planner ....0-471-37741-4 / $49.95
☐ The Continuum of Care Treatment Planner ....0-471-19568-5 / $49.95
☐ The Behavioral Medicine Treatment Planner...0-471-31923-6 / $49.95
☐ The Mental Retardation and Developmental Disability Treatment Planner ....0-471-38253-1 / $49.95
☐ The Special Education Treatment Planner...0-471-38872-6 / $49.95
☐ The Severe and Persistent Mental Illness Treatment Planner...............................0-471-35945-9 / $49.95
☐ The Personality Disorders Treatment Planner ....0-471-39403-3 / $49.95
☐ The Rehabilitation Psychology Treatment Planner ....0-471-35178-4 / $49.95
☐ The Pastoral Counseling Treatment Planner..0-471-25416-9 / $49.95
☐ The Juvenile Justice and Residential Care Treatment Planner ....0-471-43320-9 / $49.95
☐ The School Counseling and School Social Work Treatment Planner ....0-471-08496-4 / $49.95
☐ The Psychopharmacology Treatment Planner ....0-471-43322-5 / $49.95
☐ The Probation and Parole Treatment Planner..0-471-20244-4 / $49.95
☐ The Suicide and Homicide Risk Assessment and Prevention Treatment Planner ...0-471-46631-X / $49.95
☐ The Speech-Language Pathology Treatment Planner..0-471-27504-2 / $49.95
☐ The College Student Counseling Treatment Planner ....0-471-46708-1 / $49.95
☐ The Parenting Skills Treatment Planner ....0-471-48183-1 / $49.95
☐ The Early Childhood Education Intervention Treatment Planner ....0-471-65962-2 / $49.95
☐ The Co-Occurring Disorders Treatment Planner..0-471-73081-5 / $49.95
☐ The Sexual Abuse Victim and Sexual Offender Treatment Planner ....0-471-21979-7 / $49.95
☐ The Complete Women's Psychotherapy Treatment Planner ....0-470-03983-3 / $49.95

The **Complete Treatment and Homework Planners** series of books combines our bestselling *Treatment Planners* and *Homework Planners* into one easy-to-use, all-in-one resource for mental health professionals treating clients suffering from the most commonly diagnosed disorders.

☐ The Complete Depression Treatment and Homework Planner ....0-471-64515-X / $39.95
☐ The Complete Anxiety Treatment and Homework Planner ....0-471-64548-6 / $39.95

Over 500,000 Practice*Planners* sold ... ⓦ**WILEY**

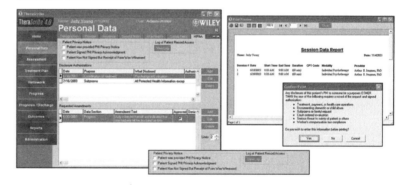

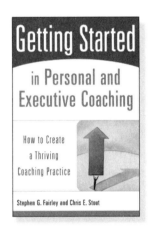
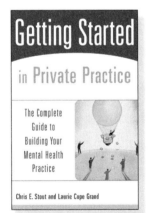

The Complete Women's Psychotherapy Treatment Planner

Practice*Planners*® Series

Treatment Planners

The Complete Adult Psychotherapy Treatment Planner, Fourth Edition
The Child Psychotherapy Treatment Planner, Fourth Edition
The Adolescent Psychotherapy Treatment Planner, Fourth Edition
The Addiction Treatment Planner, Third Edition
The Continuum of Care Treatment Planner
The Couples Psychotherapy Treatment Planner
The Employee Assistance Treatment Planner
The Pastoral Counseling Treatment Planner
The Older Adult Psychotherapy Treatment Planner
The Behavioral Medicine Treatment Planner
The Group Therapy Treatment Planner
The Gay and Lesbian Psychotherapy Treatment Planner
The Family Therapy Treatment Planner
The Severe and Persistent Mental Illness Treatment Planner
The Mental Retardation and Developmental Disability Treatment Planner
The Social Work and Human Services Treatment Planner
The Crisis Counseling and Traumatic Events Treatment Planner
The Personality Disorders Treatment Planner
The Rehabilitation Psychology Treatment Planner
The Special Education Treatment Planner
The Juvenile Justice and Residential Care Treatment Planner
The School Counseling and School Social Work Treatment Planner
The Sexual Abuse Victim and Sexual Offender Treatment Planner
The Probation and Parole Treatment Planner
The Psychopharmacology Treatment Planner
The Speech-Language Pathology Treatment Planner
The Suicide and Homicide Treatment Planner
The College Student Counseling Treatment Planner
The Parenting Skills Treatment Planner
The Early Childhood Intervention Treatment Planner
The Co-Occurring Disorders Treatment Planner
The Complete Women's Psychotherapy Treatment Planner

Progress Note Planners

The Child Psychotherapy Progress Notes Planner, Third Edition
The Adolescent Psychotherapy Progress Notes Planner, Third Edition
The Adult Psychotherapy Progress Notes Planner, Third Edition
The Addiction Progress Notes Planner, Second Edition
The Severe and Persistent Mental Illness Progress Notes Planner
The Couples Psychotherapy Progress Notes Planner
The Family Therapy Progress Notes Planner

Homework Planners

Brief Couples Therapy Homework Planner
Brief Employee Assistance Homework Planner
Brief Family Therapy Homework Planner
Grief Counseling Homework Planner
Group Therapy Homework Planner
Divorce Counseling Homework Planner
School Counseling and School Social Work Homework Planner
Child Therapy Activity and Homework Planner
Addiction Treatment Homework Planner, Third Edition
Adolescent Psychotherapy Homework Planner II
Adolescent Psychotherapy Homework Planner, Second Edition
Adult Psychotherapy Homework Planner, Second Edition
Child Psychotherapy Homework Planner, Second Edition
Parenting Skills Homework Planner

Client Education Handout Planners

Adult Client Education Handout Planner
Child and Adolescent Client Education Handout Planner
Couples and Family Client Education Handout Planner

Complete Planners

The Complete Depression Treatment and Homework Planner
The Complete Anxiety Treatment and Homework Planner

PracticePlanners®

Arthur E. Jongsma, Jr., Series Editor

The Complete Women's Psychotherapy Treatment Planner

Julie R. Ancis

Arthur E. Jongsma, Jr.

BICENTENNIAL
1807
WILEY
2007
BICENTENNIAL

JOHN WILEY & SONS, INC.

For general information on our other products and services please contact our Customer Care Department within the U.S. at (800) 762-2974, outside the United States at (317) 572-3993 or fax (317) 572-4002.

Wiley also publishes its books in a variety of electronic formats. Some content that appears in print may not be available in electronic books. For more information about Wiley products, visit our web site at www.wiley.com.

ISBN-13: 978-0-470-03983-0

Printed in the United States of America.

10 9 8 7 6 5 4 3 2 1

To Sylvie, may you always be healthy, strong, joyful, and wise. I love you.

—Julie R. Ancis

To Dr. Susan Zonnebelt-Smeenge, my good friend, an insightful author, a compassionate counselor, and an assertive female role model who understands the issues women face.

—Arthur E. Jongsma, Jr.

CONTENTS

PRACTICE*PLANNERS*® SERIES PREFACE

Accountability is an important dimension of the practice of psychotherapy. Treatment programs, public agencies, clinics, and practitioners must justify and document their treatment plans to outside review entities in order to be reimbursed for services. The books and software in the Practice*Planners*® series are designed to help practitioners fulfill these documentation requirements efficiently and professionally.

The Practice*Planners*® series includes a wide array of treatment-planning books, including not only the original *Complete Adult Psychotherapy Treatment Planner*, *Child Psychotherapy Treatment Planner*, and *Adolescent Psychotherapy Treatment Planner*, all now in their fourth editions, but also *Treatment Planners* targeted to a wide range of specialty areas of practice, including:

- Addictions
- Behavioral medicine
- College students
- Co-occurring disorders
- Couples therapy
- Crisis counseling
- Early childhood education
- Employee assistance
- Family therapy
- Gays and lesbians
- Group therapy
- Juvenile justice and residential care
- Mental retardation and developmental disability
- Neuropsychology
- Older adults
- Parenting skills
- Pastoral counseling
- Personality disorders

- Probation and parole
- Psychopharmacology
- School counseling
- Severe and persistent mental illness
- Sexual abuse victims and offenders
- Special education
- Suicide and homicide risk assessment

In addition, there are three branches of companion books that can be used in conjunction with the *Treatment Planners*, or on their own:

- *Progress Notes Planners* provide a menu of progress statements that elaborate on the client's symptom presentation and the provider's therapeutic intervention. Each *Progress Notes Planner* statement is directly integrated with the behavioral definitions and therapeutic interventions from its companion *Treatment Planner*.
- *Homework Planners* include homework assignments designed around each presenting problem (e.g., anxiety, depression, chemical dependence, anger management, eating disorders, or panic disorder) that is the focus of a chapter in its corresponding *Treatment Planner*.
- *Client Education Handout Planners* provide brochures and handouts to help educate and inform clients on presenting problems and mental health issues, as well as life skills techniques. The handouts are included on CD-ROMs for easy printing from your computer and are ideal for use in waiting rooms, at presentations, as newsletters, or as information for clients struggling with mental illness issues. The topics covered by these handouts correspond to the presenting problems in the *Treatment Planners*.

The series also includes:

- **Thera*Scribe*®,** the best selling treatment-planning and clinical record-keeping software system for mental health professionals. Thera*Scribe*® allows the user to import the data from any of the *Treatment Planner, Progress Notes Planner,* or *Homework Planner* books into the software's expandable database to simply point and click to create a detailed, organized, individualized, and customized treatment plan along with optional integrated progress notes and homework assignments.

Adjunctive books, such as *The Psychotherapy Documentation Primer* and *The Clinical Documentation Sourcebook* contain forms and resources to aid the clinician in mental health practice management.

The goal of our series is to provide practitioners with the resources they need in order to provide high quality care in the era of accountability. To put it simply: We seek to help you spend more time on patients, and less time on paperwork.

ARTHUR E. JONGSMA JR.
Grand Rapids, Michigan

ACKNOWLEDGMENTS

I express my appreciation to my mother, Helen Ancis, who has been a model of fortitude and courage and to my dear father, Joseph A. Ancis. May your memory be for a blessing.

I would like to acknowledge my co-authors whose input has enriched this treatment planner. They are all intelligent and productive individuals who have contributed and will continue to contribute to the important work on women. They include: Ekta Aulakh, Telsie A. Davis, Jana E. Frances-Fischer, Danica G. Hays, Wendy Heath-Gainer, Karia Kelch-Oliver, Anneliese A. Singh, and Wendi S. Williams.

Thank you to David Bernstein for the initial conversation about developing a Women's Treatment Planner; a conversation that resulted in its completion. He was always available to discuss direction and logistics of the planner and remained committed to its quality. Thank you to Art Jongsma for his vision and openness to varied perspectives. I also appreciate the helpful and responsive staff at Wiley. Thank you to Sue Rhoda, Art Jongsma's manuscript manager.

I wish to express my gratitude to all of the women and men in my life who are models of advocacy and good will. My friends, J. Ashby, M. Cohen, D. and M. Goldstein, J. Hill, G. Iovinella, E. Joseph, R. Kern, N. Ladany, D. Lee, T. Morgan, and A. Podolsky. Thank you all for your patience, good humor, insights, and support. Your lives validate the need for interventions responsive to women's needs. Thank you to R. Moshe Parnes for his listening with intention, warmth, guidance, and support during the past two years and for paving the way for developing a greater appreciation of Hashem. What a gift. Thank you also to the Parnes family for making that possible.

Thank you to my colleagues and students at Georgia State University who make coming to work a pleasant experience.

To those who work to better the multitude of systems that often perpetuate trauma and other ills, you have my appreciation and admiration.

JRA

I am indebted to Dr. Julie Ancis and the colleagues that assisted her for the female perspective they brought to this *Women's Issues Psychotherapy Treatment Planner*. They consistently examined the function of culture and society in imposing unique roles and expectations on women. They were sensitive to the emotional conflict that these expectations may generate and suggested coping skills as Interventions to overcome these conflicts. Thank you for your good work, Julie.

I also want to thank my wonderful team at John Wiley & Sons: Peggy, David, Alicia, Judi, Lynne, and Micheline. They are all first-class professionals and have supported the Practice*Planner*® series with fresh enthusiasm for over 10 years.

Finally, my manuscript manager, Sue Rhoda, plays a critical role in keeping the project moving forward with her wonderful organization and word-processing skills. She brings order out of chaos time after time. Thank you, Sue!

AEJ

INTRODUCTION

PLANNER FOCUS

The field of counseling and psychology has witnessed increased attention to women's issues and, more generally, to the role of gender in influencing our attitudes, worldview, and experiences. In 1978, the Division of Counseling Psychology of the American Psychological Association (APA) approved the "Principies Concerning the Counseling and Psychotherapy of Women" developed by the Division 17 Ad Hoc Committee on Women. These Principles were subsequently endorsed by American Psychological Association Divisions 12, 16, 29, and 35, expanded, and published in 1986. Under the direction of an American Psychological Association Task Force headed by Carol Enns, Roberta Nutt, and Joy Rice, new *Guidelines for Psychological Practice with Girls and Women* are currently in progress and include components related to professional responsibility and practice applications. The first author of this *Women's Issues Psychotherapy Treatment Planner*, Julie Ancis, served as chair of the Diversity Section of the American Psychological Association Task Force.

Women continue to have higher rates of general and mental healthcare utilization in relation to men (medical letter on the CDC and FDA, 2003; Rhodes, Goering, To, and Williams, 2002). While clinical literature related to specific groups of women and women in general is accessible, practitioners often lack knowledge of women's presenting issues or of relevant interventions. Several authors have described the gender bias that continues to pervade traditional approaches to assessment, diagnosis, and interventions (American Psychological

Association, 2006; Ballou and Brown, 2002; Caplan and Cosgrove, 2004; Worell and Remer, 2003). Earlier research demonstrated the existence of gender-role stereotyping by counselors in training and therapists (Broverman, Broverman, Clarkson, Rosenkrantz, and Vogel, 1970; Dreman, 1978; Hampton, Lambert, and Snell, 1986). More recent studies have demonstrated gender-typing among psychotherapists (Crosby & Sprock, 2004; Turner and Turner, 1991) and mental health professional's tendency to judge female clients as less competent to understand counseling and to give informed consent than male clients (Danzinger and Welfel, 2000). Gender bias in the diagnosis of personality disorders has been demonstrated in several studies that reveal that clinicians differentially diagnose male and female subjects exhibiting identical symptomatology (Becker and Lamb, 1994; Cosgrove, 2004; Ford and Widiger, 1989; Hamilton, Rothbart, and Dawes, 1986; Morey and Ochoa, 1989). For example, females are significantly more likely to be categorized as histrionic and borderline than males exhibiting identical symptoms (Becker and Lamb, 1994; Ford and Widiger, 1989; Hamilton, Rothbart, and Dawes, 1986). Similarly, therapists seem to diagnose depression more frequently in women who meet the standardized criteria than in men and fail to identify men who do not fit feminine expectations for depression. Among those who do not certify as depressed with standard testing, false positives are more common in women than men (Potts, Burnman, and Wells, 1991).

Gender bias in counseling is often not direct. Rather, the more subtle omission of important components of gender-fair therapy has been found, such as fostering traditional roles, not accepting women's anger, and lack of consideration of the sociocultural context of problems (Ancis and Sanchez-Hucles, 2000; Matlin, 2000; Sesan, 1988).

Women evidence specific needs and problems compared to their male counterparts. Effective clinical practice with women requires consid-eration of their specific challenges, external stresses, their social and cultural context, and related psychological impact. For example, most women (69%) are exposed to a traumatic stressor in their lifetime (Resnick, Kilpatrick, Dansky, Saunders, and Bets, 1993). Twenty-five percent of women compared to 8% of men report being raped or physically assaulted by a spouse, partner, or date in their lifetime (Tjaden and Thoennes, 2000). These issues have significant psychological implications. Several studies have demonstrated a significant relationship between experiences with sexism and poorer mental health among women (e.g., Klonoff, Landrine, and Campbell, 2000; Koss, Bailey, Yan, Herrera, and Lichter, 2003; Moradi and Subich, 2002; Szymanski, 2005). For example, rape and domestic violence seem to account for a higher prevalence of trauma in women, and survivors have higher rates of

Posttraumatic Stress Disorder (Tjaden and Thoennes, 2000). The rising incidence of eating disorders among women is associated with increased media attention to the appearance of women, coupled with the relatively narrow standard of beauty in Western society (Posvac, Posvac, and Weigel, 2001). Taylor, Henderson, and Jackson (1991) found that life stress, physical health problems, and internalized racism were significant predictors of depressive symptoms in African American women. Inattention to contextual issues such as discrimination, life stress, acculturative stress, poverty, and gender role socialization and their impact on personal and social functioning (APA, 2004) may contribute to the lack of recognition of women's problems such as domestic violence, the underdiagnosis of or double standards about problems such as alcohol abuse (Collins, 2002), and an inappropriate focus on intrapsychic factors (Ancis, 2004).

Related to an understanding of the role that discrimination and other life stressors, competent assessment and counseling with women requires an understanding of the client's cultural framework. This requires attention to the intersections of cultural influences; identity development in relation to gender, race, ethnicity, sexual orientation, religion, and socioeconomic conditions; and the presenting problem. Cultural factors influence how distress is experienced, expressed, and explained, as well as the client's response to treatment (Ancis, 2004; Kirmayer, 2001). For example, culture, ethnicity, and acculturation level has been found to influence the expression and attribution of depression among women (Brown, Abe-Kin, and Barrio, 2003). An association between somatic expression, psychiatric stigma, and depression has been recorded in countries such as India and Saudi Arabia (see Kleinman, 1988). Disruptive symptoms have been attributed to metaphysical causes such as loss of the soul, spirit possession (Koss-Chioino, 1992), or shameful causes such as past family transgressions or personal weakness (Gong-Guy, Cravens, and Patterson, 1991). Researchers have also described various culturally recognized syndromes that appear to correspond closely with the diagnosis of Major Depressive Disorder and anxiety among women (Lin et al., 1992).

The chapters in *The Complete Women's Psychotherapy Treatment Planner* include prevalent presenting concerns among women, including depression, anxiety, career success obstacles, body image disturbance /eating disorders, childbearing decisions, balancing work and family /multiple roles, domestic violence, sexual assault and rape, partner relational problems, and infertility. Contextual and cultural factors that have been identified among diverse women are integrated into problem definition, goals, objectives, and interventions. These include the experience of discrimination and oppression and associated anger, anxiety, depression, passivity, and shame; culturally influenced beliefs and practices; the importance of family and connection with the community; and the role of spirituality as an aspect of psychological well-being and coping (Ancis, 2004; Comas-Díaz, 1992).

Theoretical approaches and interventions that are particularly facilitative to women in general and to particular subgroups of women have been described in the literature (Alexander, Neimeyer, and Follette, 1991; Comas-Díaz and Greene, 1994; Fitzgerald and Nutt, 1986; Foa and Street, 2001; Gilbert, 1980; Jackson and Greene, 2000; Kubany, Hill, and Owens, 2003; Stein et al., 2001; Wilson, Fairburn, Agras, Walsh, and Kraemer, 2002). *The Planner* outlines goals, objectives, and interventions that are particularly efficacious to women's mental health and are associated with positive outcomes. Many of these approaches consider culture, gender, race, ethnicity, class, sexual orientation, and other identities within a historical and sociopolitical context (Ancis, 2004). Also, consideration is given to the contribution of structural factors to women's distress, rather than an exclusive focus on individual pathology. Interventions include cognitive-behavioral approaches, as well as strategies consistent with research on diverse women's mental health. In the case of eating disorders, therapies that teach clients to modify negative internalized self-attitudes and expectations about body size have been found to be effective (Wilson, Fairburn, Argras, Walsh, and Kramer, 2002). For survivors of domestic abuse and sexual abuse, positive outcomes are associated with therapies that help women cope with trauma-related memories, reduce negative self-talk, and change their distorted sense of responsibility for trauma (Foa and Street, 2001; Kubany, Hill, and Owens, 2003). Interventions such as stress management techniques, relaxation training, and psychoeducation are recommended for increasing women's control of symptoms and coping effectively with physical and psychological pain for women facing health challenges (Altmaier et al., 2003). Relatedly, research indicates that optimal and effective treatment with women is facilitated when clinicians implement interventions that encourage the development of protective factors such as self-efficacy and problem-solving skills, reframe women's concerns from a coping and ecological perspective, and emphasize a strength perspective in practice.

AUDIENCE

The Complete Women's Psychotherapy Treatment Planner has been written for mental health professionals, including counselors, social workers, psychologists, and psychiatrists who work with women clients.

In addition, supervisors in clinical settings and instructors who teach courses in the psychology of women, the psychology of gender, and clinical practicum and internship in counseling, psychology, social work, and psychiatry would benefit from this *Planner*.

ABOUT PRACTICE*PLANNERS*® TREATMENT PLANNERS

Pressure from third-party payors, accrediting agencies, and other outside parties has increased the need for clinicians to quickly produce effective, high-quality treatment plans. *Treatment Planners* provide all the elements necessary to quickly and easily develop formal treatments plans that satisfy the needs of most third-party payors and state and federal review agencies.

Each Treatment Planner:

- Saves you hours of time-consuming paperwork.
- Offers the freedom to develop customized treatment plans.
- Includes over 1,000 clear statements describing the behavioral manifestations of each relational problem, and includes long-term goals, short-term objectives, and clinically tested treatment options.
- Has an easy-to-use reference format that helps locate treatment plan components by behavioral problem or *DSM-IV*™ diagnosis.

As with the rest of the books in the Practice*Planners*® series, our aim is to clarify, simplify, and accelerate the treatment planning process, so you spend less time on paperwork, and more time with your clients.

HOW TO USE THIS TREATMENT PLANNER

Use this *Treatment Planner* to write treatment plans according to the following progression of six steps:

1. **Problem Selection.** Although the client may discuss a variety of issues during the assessment, the clinician must determine the most significant problems on which to focus the treatment process. Usually a primary problem will surface, and secondary problems may also be evident. Some other problems may have to be set aside as not urgent enough to require treatment at this time. An effective treatment plan can only deal with a few selected problems or treatment will lose its direction. Choose the problem within this *Planner* that most accurately represents your client's presenting issues.

2. **Problem Definition.** Each client presents with unique nuances as to how a problem behaviorally reveals itself in her life. Therefore, each problem that is selected for treatment focus requires a specific definition about how it is evidenced in the particular client. The symptom pattern should be associated with diagnostic criteria and codes such as those found in the *DSM-IV* or the *International Classification of Diseases*. This *Planner* offers such behaviorally specific definition statements to choose from or to serve as a model for your own personally crafted statements.

3. **Goal Development.** The next step in developing your treatment plan is to set broad goals for the resolution of the target problem. These statements need not be crafted in measurable terms, but can be global, long-term goals that indicate a desired positive outcome to the treatment procedures. This *Planner* provides several possible goal statements for each problem, but one statement is all that is required in a treatment plan.

4. **Objective Construction.** In contrast to long-term goals, objectives must be stated in behaviorally measurable or observable language so that it is clear to review agencies, health maintenance organizations, and managed care organizations when the client has achieved the established objectives. The objectives presented in this *Planner* are designed to meet this demand for accountability. Numerous alternatives are presented to allow construction of a variety of treatment plan possibilities for the same presenting problem.

5. **Intervention Creation.** Interventions are the actions of the clinician designed to help the client complete the objectives. There should be at least one intervention for every objective. If the client does not accomplish the objective after the initial intervention, new interventions should be added to the plan. Interventions should be selected on the basis of the client's needs and strengths as well as the treatment provider's full therapeutic repertoire. This *Planner* contains interventions from a broad range of therapeutic approaches, and we encourage the provider to write other interventions reflecting his or her own training and experience.

Some suggested interventions listed in the *Planner* refer to specific books that can be assigned to the client for adjunctive bibliotherapy. Appendix A contains a full bibliographic reference list of these materials, including these two popular choices: *Read Two Books and Let's Talk Next Week: Using Bibliotherapy in Clinical Practice* (2000) by Maidman and DiMenna and *Rent Two Films and Let's Talk in the Morning: Using Popular Movies in Psychotherapy,* 2nd ed. (2001) by Hesley and Hesley (both books are published by

Wiley). For further information about self-help books, mental health professionals may wish to consult *The Authoritative Guide to Self-Help Resources in Mental Health,* revised ed. (2003) by Norcross et al. (available from Guilford Press, New York).

6. **Diagnosis Determination.**   The determination of an appropriate diagnosis is based on an evaluation of the client's complete clinical presentation. The clinician must compare the behavioral, cognitive, emotional, and interpersonal symptoms that the client presents with the criteria for diagnosis of a mental illness condition as described in *DSM-IV*. Despite arguments made against diagnosing clients in this manner, diagnosis is a reality that exists in the world of mental health care, and it is a necessity for third-party reimbursement. It is the clinician's thorough knowledge of *DSM-IV* criteria and a complete understanding of the client assessment data that contribute to the most reliable, valid diagnosis.

Congratulations! After completing these six steps, you should have a comprehensive and individualized treatment plan ready for immediate implementation and presentation to the client. A sample treatment plan for Balancing Work and Family/Multiple Roles is provided at the end of this introduction.

FINAL NOTE ON TAILORING THE TREATMENT PLAN TO THE CLIENT

One important aspect of effective treatment planning is that each plan should be tailored to the individual client's problems and needs. Treatment plans should not be mass produced, even if clients have similar problems. The individual's strengths and weaknesses, unique stressors, social network, family circumstances, and symptom patterns must be considered in developing a treatment strategy. Drawing on our own years of clinical experience, we have put together a variety of treatment choices. These statements can be combined in thousands of permutations to develop detailed treatment plans. Relying on their own good judgment, clinicians can easily select the statements that are appropriate for the individuals whom they are treating. In addition, we encourage readers to add their own definitions, goals, objectives, and interventions to the existing samples. As with all of the books in the *Treatment Planners* series, it is our hope that this book will help promote effective, creative treatment planning—a process that will ultimately benefit the client, clinician, and mental health community.

SAMPLE TREATMENT PLAN

BALANCING WORK AND FAMILY/MULTIPLE ROLES

Definitions: Experiences stress associated with balancing the multiple tasks associated with motherhood and work roles.

Describes stress and anxiety associated with cumulative demands of multiple roles.

Experiences fatigue and difficulty concentrating (e.g., feeling over-whelmed) due to role overload.

Experiences partner relationship strain and dissatisfaction due to inequitable division of responsibilities.

Goals: Develop a realistic perspective regarding demands and obligations of multiple roles and their completion.

Develop a support system to assist with multiple roles and responsibilities.

Maintain a balance between the multiple demands of motherhood, work, and other life roles and responsibilities.

OBJECTIVES

1. Describe role and responsibilities associated with work and family and related thoughts, feelings, and behaviors.

2. Describe at least three expectations related to work and family obligations and their relationship to gender role socialization and emotional conflict.

INTERVENTIONS

1. Explore with the client her multiple roles and responsibilities associated with work and family; clarify related thoughts and feelings.

1. Explore with the client her expectations regarding the balance between work and family, and discuss how this relates to internalized gender role stereotypes.

2. Discuss the client's potential feelings and guilt, shame, and anxiety

associated with not meeting internal or external expectations.

3. Identify and replace internalized expectations and standards regarding multiple roles that are potentially harmful.

1. Assist the client with identifying those expectations that are helpful and those that are potentially harmful; help the client discard those that are causing undue stress and strain and replace them with more realistic messages.

4. Clarify values and priorities.

1. Help the client to explore and clarify her own values and priorities; encourage her to reduce the psychological importance placed on one or more roles to reduce the level of conflict.

5. Learn and implement problem-solving and conflict-resolution skills.

1. Use behavioral techniques (i.e., education, modeling, role-playing, corrective feedback, positive reinforcement) to teach the couple problem-solving and conflict-resolution skills including defining the problem constructively and specifically, brainstorming options, evaluating options, compromise, choosing options and implementing a plan, and evaluating the results.

2. Assign the couple a homework exercise to use

and record newly learned problem-solving and conflict-resolution skills (or assign "Applying Problem-Solving to Interpersonal Conflict" in the *Adult Psychotherapy Homework Planner,* 2nd ed. by Jongsma); process results in session.

6. Contract with three to five friends and family members who will assume active support.

1. Facilitate the client's development of a social support network to assist with multiple roles and responsibilities; develop a list of active support behaviors (e.g., babysitting, help with cleaning).

7. Generate a list of self-care activities and make a commitment to regularly participate in such activities.

1. Explore potential self-care activities and encourage the client's participation (or assign "Identify and Schedule Pleasant Activities" in the *Adult Psychotherapy Homework Planner,* 2nd ed. by Jongsma).

Diagnosis: 309.28   Adjustment Disorder with Mixed Anxiety and Depressed Mood

INTRODUCTION REFERENCES

Alexander, P. C., Neimeyer, R. A., and Follette, V. M. (1991). Group therapy for women sexually abused as children: A controlled study and investigation of individual differences. *Journal of Interpersonal Violence, 6,* 218–231.

Altmaier, E. M., Fraley, S. S., Homaifar, B.Y., Maloney, R., Rasheed, S., and Rippentrop, A. E. (2003). Health counseling: Assessment and intervention. In

M. Kopala and M. E. Keitel (Eds.), *Handbook of Counseling Women* (pp. 323–344). Thousand Oaks, CA: Sage.

American Psychological Association (2004). *Resolution on Culture and Gender Awareness in International Psychology.* Washington, DC: Author.

American Psychological Association (2006). *Guidelines for Psychological Practice with Girls and Women.* Manuscript submitted for publication.

Ancis, J. R. (Ed.) (2004). *Culturally Responsive Interventions: Innovative Approaches to Working with Diverse Populations.* New York: Brunner-Routledge.

Ancis, J. R., and Sanchez-Hucles, J. V. (2000). A preliminary analysis of counseling students' attitudes toward counseling women and women of color: Implications for cultural competency training. *Journal of Multicultural Counseling and Development, 28,* 16–31.

Ballou, M., and Brown, L. S. (Eds.) (2002). *Rethinking Mental Health and Disorder: Feminist Perspectives.* New York: Guilford Press.

Becker, D., and Lamb, S. (1994). Sex bias in the diagnosis of borderline personality disorder and posttraumatic stress disorder. *Professional Psychology, 25,* 55–61.

Broverman, I. K., Broverman, D. M., Clarkson, F. E., Rosenkrantz, P. S., Vogel, S. R. (1970). Sex-role stereotypes and clinical judgments of mental health. *Journal of Consulting and Clinical Psychology, 34,* 1–7.

Brown, C., Abe-Kim, J. S., and Barrio, C. (2003). Depression in ethnically diverse women: Implications for treatment in primary care settings. *Professional Psychology: Research and Practice, 34,* 10–19.

Caplan, P. J., and Cosgrove, L. (Eds.) (2004). *Bias in Psychiatric Diagnosis.* Northvale, NJ: Jason Aronson.

Collins, L. H. (2002). Alcohol and drug addiction in women: Phenomenology and prevention. In M. Ballou and L. S. Brown (Eds.), *Rethinking Mental Health and Disorder: Feminist Perspectives* (pp. 198–230). New York: Guilford Press.

Comas-Díaz, L. (1992). The future of psychotherapy with ethnic minorities. *Psychotherapy: Theory, Research, and Practice, 29*(1), 88–94.

Comas-Díaz, L., and Greene, B. (Eds.) (1994). *Women of Color: Integrating Ethnic and Gender Identities in Psychotherapy.* New York: Guilford Press.

Cosgrove, L. (2004). Gender bias and sex distribution of mental disorders in the *DSM-IV-TR.* In P. J. Caplan and L. Cosgrove (Eds.), *Bias in Psychiatric Diagnosis* (pp. 127–140). Northvale, NJ: Jason Aronson.

Crosby, J. P., and Sprock, J. (2004). Effect of patient sex, clinician sex, and sex role on the diagnosis of antisocial personality disorder: Models of underpathologizing and overpathologizing biases. *Journal of Clinical Psychology, 60,* 583–604.

Danzinger, P. R., and Welfel, E. R. (2000). Age, gender and health bias in counselors: An empirical analysis. *Journal of Mental Health Counseling, 22*(2), 135–149.

Dremen, S. B. (1978). Sex-role stereotyping in mental health standards in Israel. *Journal of Clinical Psychology, 34,* 961–966.

Fitzgerald, L. F., and Nutt, R. (1986). The Division 17 Principles concerning the counseling/psychotherapy of women: Rationale and implementation. *The Counseling Psychologist, 14,* 180–216.

Foa, E. B., and Street, G. P. (2001). Women and traumatic events. *Journal of Clinical Psychiatry, 62* (Suppl. 17), 29–34.

Ford, M. R., and Widiger, T. A. (1989). Sex bias in the diagnosis of histrionic and antisocial personality disorders. *Journal of Consulting and Clinical Psychology, 37,* 301–305.

Gilbert, L. A. (1980). Feminist therapy. In A. M. Brodsky and R. T. Hare-Mustin (Eds.), *Women and Psychotherapy: An Assessment of Research and Practice* (pp. 245–265). New York: Guilford Press.

Gong-Guy, E., Cravens, R. B., and Patterson, T. E. (1991). Clinical issues of mental health service delivery to refugees. *American Psychologist, 46,* 642–648.

Hamilton, S., Rothbart, M., and Dawes, R. M. (1986). Sex bias, diagnosis, and *DSM-III. Sex Roles, 15,* 269–274.

Hampton, B., Lambert, F. B., and Snell, W. E. (1986). Therapists' judgments of mentally healthy beliefs for women and men. *Journal of Rational-Emotive Therapy, 4*(2), 169–179.

Hesley, J., and Hesley, J. (2001). *Rent Two Films and Let's Talk in the Morning: Using Popular Movies in Psychotherapy,* 2nd ed. New York: John Wiley & Sons.

Jackson, L. C., and Greene, B. (Eds.) (2000). *Psychotherapy with African American Women: Innovations in Psychodynamic Perspectives and Practice.* New York: Guilford Press.

Joshua, J. Maidman, and DiMenna, D. (2000). *Read Two Books and Let's Talk Next Week: Using Bibliotherapy in Clinical Practice.* New York: John Wiley & Sons.

Kirmayer, L. J. (2001). Cultural variations in the clinical presentation of depression anxiety: Implications for diagnosis and treatment. *Journal of Clinical Psychology, 62,* 22–28.

Kleinman, A. (1988). *Rethinking Psychiatry: From Cultural Category to Personal Experience.* New York: Free Press.

Klonoff, E. A., Landrine, H., and Campbell, R. (2000). Sexist discrimination may account for well-known gender differences in psychiatric symptoms. *Psychology of Women Quarterly, 24,* 93–99.

Koss, M. P., Bailey, J. A., Yan, N. P., Herrera, V. M., and Lichter, E. L. (2003). Depression and PTSD in survivors of male violence: Research and training initiatives to facilitate recovery. *Psychology of Women Quarterly, 27,* 130–142.

Koss-Chioino, J. (1992). *Women as Healers, Women as Patients: Mental Health Care and Traditional Healing in Puerto Rico.* Boulder, CO: Westview Press.

Kubany, E. S., Hill, E. E., and Owens, J. A. (2003). Cognitive trauma therapy for battered women with PTSD: Preliminary findings. *Journal of Traumatic Stress, 16,* 81–91.

Lin, K. M., Lau, J. K., Yamamoto, J., Zheng, Y. P., Kim, H. S., Cho, K. H. and Nakasaki, G. (1992). Hwa-byung: A community study of Korean Americans. *Journal of Nervous and Mental Disease, 180 (6),* 386–391.

Matlin, M. W. (2000). *The Psychology of Women,* 4th ed. Fort Worth, TX: Harcourt.

Moradi, B., and Subich, L. M. (2002). Perceived sexist events and feminist identity development attitudes: Links to women's psychological distress. *The Counseling Psychologist, 30,* 44–65.

Morey, L., and Ochoa, E. (1989). An investigation of adherence to diagnostic criteria: Clinical diagnosis of the *DSM-III* personality disorders. *Journal of Personality Disorders, 3,* 180–192.

Norcross, J. C., Santrock, J. W., Campbell, L. F., Smith, T. P., Sommer, R., and Zuckerman, E. L. (2003) *The Authoritative Guide to Self-Help Resources in Mental Health,* rev. ed. New York: Guilford.

Posvac, H., Posvac, S., and Weigel, R. (2001). Reducing the impact of media images on women at risk for body image disturbance: Three targeted interventions. *Journal of Social and Clinical Psychology, 20,* 324–331.

Potts, M. K., Burnam, M. A., Wells, K. B. (1991). Gender differences in depression detection: A comparison of clinical diagnosis and standardized assessment. *Psychological Assessment: A Journal of Consulting and Clinical Psychology, 3,* 609–615.

Resnick, H. S., Kilpatrick, D. G., Dansky, B. S., Saunders, B. E., and Best, C. L. (1993). Prevalence of civilian trauma and posttraumatic stress disorder in a representative national sample of women. *Journal of Consulting and Clinical Psychology, 61,* 984–991.

Rhodes, A. E., Goering, P. N., To, T., and Williams, J. I. (2002). Gender and outpatient mental health service use. *Social Science and Medicine, 54,* 1–10.

Sesan, R. (1988). Sex bias and sex-role stereotyping in psychotherapy with women: Survey results. *Psychotherapy, 25,* 107–116.

Stein, R. I., Saelens, B. E., Dounchis, J. Z., Lewczyk, C. M., Swenson, A. A., and Wilfley, D. E. (2001). Treatment of eating disorders in women. *The Counseling Psychologist, 29,* 695–732.

Szymanski, D. M. (2005). Heterosexism and sexism as correlates of psychological distress in lesbians. *Journal of Counseling and Development, 83,* 355–360.

Taylor, J., Henderson, D. and Jackson, B. B. (1991). A holistic model for understanding and predicting depressive symptoms in African American women. *Journal of Community Psychology, 19,* 306–321.

Tjaden, P., and Thoennes, N. (2000). *Full Report of the Prevalence, Incidence, and Consequences of Violence Against Women: Findings from the National Violence Against Women Survey.* Washington, DC: U.S. Department of Justice.

Turner, B. F., and Turner, C. B. (1991). BEM sex-role inventory stereotypes for men and women varying in age and race among National Register psychologists. *Psychological Reports, 69,* 931–944.

Weeks, M. (2003, April). *NIMH Launches First Public Education Campaign to Reach More Than 6 Million Men.* Medical letter on the CDC and FDA, 6–7.

Wilson, G. T., Fairburn, C. C., Agras, W. S., Walsh, B. T., and Kraemer, H. (2002). Cognitive–behavior therapy for bulimia nervosa: Time course and mechanisms of change. *Journal of Consulting and Clinical Psychology, 67,* 451–459.

Worell, J., and Remer, P. (2003). *Feminist Perspectives in Therapy: Empowering Diverse Women,* 2nd ed. New York: John Wiley & Sons.

ANXIETY

Chapter co-authored with Wendy Heath-Gainer, EdS

BEHAVIORAL DEFINITIONS

1. Describes an overwhelming and persistent sense of worry and fear about a number of events or circumstances.
2. Exhibits physical symptoms, which may include sweating, raised blood pressure, fast heart rate, palpitations, rapid breathing, increased muscle tension, shakiness, fatigue, dry mouth, trouble swallowing, nausea, or diarrhea.
3. Evidences sleep disturbance, often with difficulty falling asleep, waking in the night without being able to go back to sleep, or restless unsatisfying sleep.
4. Displays feelings of irritability, being on edge, and/or restlessness.
5. Experiences difficulty concentrating or mind going blank.
6. Feels immobilized or may completely withdraw in response to/anticipation of a real or imagined danger.

—. _____
    _____
—. _____
    _____
—. _____
    _____

LONG-TERM GOALS

1. Increase overall sense of well-being via reduction/elimination of anxiety.
2. Resolve the core conflict that is the source of anxiety.
3. Address and eliminate maladaptive thought processes that lead to anxious responses.

4. Resolve issues involving low self-esteem or low self-efficacy that contribute to anxiety.

5. Recognize the role of precipitating factors such as social oppression, gender roles, prior trauma, and learned behavior in the perpetuation of anxiety.

6. Enhance ability to handle effectively life stressors.

—. _____

_____

—. _____

_____

—. _____

_____

SHORT-TERM OBJECTIVES

1. Verbalize anxiety symptoms as well as when, where, and how frequently they occur; describe attempts to resolve anxiety. (1)

2. Identify precipitating events, thoughts, feelings, and reactions that are believed to contribute to anxiety. (1, 2)

THERAPEUTIC INTERVENTIONS

1. Build a level of trust with the client that will facilitate an exploration of fears and patterns in her symptoms of anxiety.

1. Build a level of trust with the client that will facilitate an exploration of fears and patterns in her symptoms of anxiety.

2. Administer a standardized psychometric measure of anxiety such as the Beck Anxiety Inventory or the Personality Assessment Inventory™ (PAI™) to obtain a quantifiable measure of the severity of anxiety, and an objective and/or a standardized picture of symptom clusters; combine results with information from the interview and the client's history; review with the client.

3. Articulate the connection between anxiety in women and internal/external contributing factors. (3, 4)

3. Explore with the client her current understanding of the external and internal factors that contribute to her anxiety (e.g., gender roles, social relationships/lack of support, socioeconomic status, trauma, brain chemistry, and hormones).

4. Refer the client to sources that will deepen her understanding of the relationship between gender roles and anxiety; suggest books such as *Women's Rights in the U.S.A: Policy Debates and Gender Roles* (Stetson), *Coping With Changing Gender Roles* (Hanan), or *Gender Roles and Power* (Lipman-Blumen).

4. Implement self-care strategies that serve to augment the positive effects of other interventions. (5, 6)

5. Aid the client in devising a healthy diet and eating schedule, a pattern of adequate sleep and relaxation, as well as regular cardiovascular exercise.

6. Educate the client on the relaxing, calming, and balancing benefits of practices such as yoga, meditation, and prayer; provide suggestions on how to get started (e.g., book, video, local gym class).

5. Learn and practice methods of reducing anxiety in a variety of situations. (6, 7)

6. Educate the client on the relaxing, calming, and balancing benefits of practices such as yoga, meditation, and prayer; provide suggestions on how to get started (e.g., book, video, local gym class).

7. Train the client in the use of prescribed breathing, deep-muscle relaxation, the Relaxation Response, Systematic Desensitization, Anxiety Management Training, Stress Inoculation Training, or the

P-A-R-T model, depending on the type of anxiety exhibited and the client's preference.

6. Develop the ability to determine when the use of anxiety-reduction techniques is necessary and how to use them effectively in 9 out of 10 anxiety-arousing situations. (8, 9)

8. Using behavioral rehearsal of the anxiety-reduction techniques, assist the client in achieving mastery and applying them in real-life situations.

9. Obtain feedback on any difficulties the client experiences in application and provide tips for integrating methods into his/her everyday routine.

7. Complete a physician/psychiatrist evaluation to assess the need for medication. (10, 11)

10. Refer the client to a physician or a psychiatrist for medication consultation.

11. Monitor the client's compliance with prescribed medication, as well as her feelings about its effectiveness; confer with her physician/psychiatrist on a regular basis.

8. Comply with prescribed medications (if needed) and report any side effects to the physician/psychiatrist. (11)

11. Monitor the client's compliance with prescribed medication, as well as her feelings about its effectiveness; confer with her physician/psychiatrist on a regular basis.

9. Acknowledge underlying irrational or illogical thought patterns that contribute to anxiety. (12)

12. Elicit the client's specific patterns of thought that contribute to anxious states; aid client in understanding the connection between the identified maladaptive thoughts and anxious feelings.

10. Self-correct maladaptive thought patterns preemptively in order to lessen or eliminate anxiety at least 90% of the time; increase positive self-talk. (13, 14)

13. Educate the client on thought-stopping techniques and positive reframing in order to preempt anxious reactions.

14. Encourage the use of positive self-talk as a replacement to some

of the automatic, negative self-talk being utilized currently.

11. Attempt to focus on and recreate surroundings, situations, and mental states that have proven to be calming and low-anxiety in the past. (6, 7, 15, 16)

6. Educate the client on the relaxing, calming, and balancing benefits of practices such as yoga, meditation, and prayer; provide suggestions on how to get started (e.g., book, video, local gym class).

7. Train the client in the use of prescribed breathing, deep-muscle relaxation, the Relaxation Response, Systematic Desensitization, Anxiety Management Training, Stress Inoculation Training, or the P-A-R-T model, depending on the type of anxiety exhibited and the client's preference.

15. Educate the client on how to avoid and/or minimize anxiety-provoking stimuli and situations to the extent that this is possible.

16. Encourage the client to attend to strengths/positive experiences that will increase her focus on what has proven to be successful in the past. (e.g., spending time alone to unwind, asserting herself at work, reaching goals that she has set).

12. Identify the relationship between multiple roles, role overload, role strain, and anxiety reactions. (17)

17. Explore with the client possi-bilities for minimizing role over-load and role strain through sharing responsibilities at home and work, reducing or elimin-ating unnecessary demands, reprioritizing responsibilities, and implementing time management skills.

13. Understand the connection between low self-worth and self-efficacy, restrictive gender roles, and anxious responses. (18)

18. Facilitate the client's under-standing of the development of low self-efficacy and anxiety.

14. Begin to refer to an internal standard of performance, morals, achievement, appearance, and so on, rather than sociocultural, parental, spousal, or otherwise externally imposed judgments. (19)

15. Read materials on anxiety, including information about its origins, course, prevalence, and treatment; encourage self-help. (20)

16. Commit to a consistent course of action involving volunteering, community service, activism, further education, or other activity focused on contributing to society at least three or four times per month. (21, 22)

17. Work through any unresolved aspects of prior traumatic events and understand the impact of trauma on anxiety reactions. (23)

18. Understand specific social mores, gender roles, and expectations that have led to internal conflicts and anxious feelings. (24, 25, 26)

19. Collaborate with the client in identifying and listing her own beliefs regarding standard of performance, morals, achievement, appearance, and so on; facilitate client's use of her own internal barometer as basis for self-worth.

20. Emphasize self-education and self-help as a future coping strategy for overcoming anxiety and adverse situations. Suggest books such as *Anxiety, Phobias, & Panic: A Step-by-Step Program for Regaining Control of Your Life* (Peurifoy), or *Overcoming Anxiety: A Self-Help Guide Using Cognitive Behavioral Techniques* (Kennerley).

21. Aid the client in seeing the connection between a focus on helping others or improving society and a reduction in anxiety (i.e., dwelling on maladaptive thoughts).

22. Offer suggestions as to possible activities or causes to which the client can devote her time and expertise.

23. Identify unresolved aspects of prior traumatic events (e.g., rape, witnessing/experiencing extreme violence, natural disaster) and help the client to resolve them.

24. Explore with the client how gender roles have been received and internalized, and in turn how they have contributed to her current anxiety.

19. Verbalize the degree to which current life circumstances could be improved in areas such as work, home, and school. (27)

20. Implement steps (e.g., couples therapy, increased communication) to improve relationships deemed necessary to save or enhance; end relationships that have been deemed unsalvageable due to ongoing extreme negativity or abuse. (28)

21. Establish a support system of trusting individuals in order to discuss life stressors and help reduce anxiety. (29)

22. Retake the objective measure of anxiety that was administered at the beginning of therapy; discuss the extent to which anxiety symptoms have been reduced in severity and duration since beginning therapy. (30)

25. Provide the client with examples from the past and present of highly achieved women; encourage the client to articulate positive role models in her own life (e.g., female family members she admires, mentors).

26. Formulate with the client at least three possible solutions to resisting expectations that are limiting and anxiety producing.

27. Collaborate with the client to determine what kind of changes need to be made, internally and externally, for calmness and satisfaction to exist within the arenas of work, home, and school.

28. Devise a plan, together, to allow the client to end toxic relationships and save those that she believes are worth salvaging; role-play assertive and effective interactions with others.

29. Explore with the client avenues for receiving emotional support from others; connect her with further services such as women's groups when necessary.

30. Compare current test results to baseline scores in order to reevaluate occurrence and severity of anxiety symptoms and treatment effectiveness; review results and elicit further feedback from client regarding treatment efficacy.

—. _____   —. _____
     _____   _____
—. _____   —. _____
     _____   _____
—. _____   —. _____
     _____   _____

DIAGNOSTIC SUGGESTIONS:

Axis I: 300.02   Generalized Anxiety Disorder
300.00   Anxiety Disorder NOS
309.24   Adjustment Disorder with Anxiety
300.01   Panic Disorder without Agoraphobia
300.21   Panic Disorder with Agoraphobia
300.23   Social Phobia
308.3   Acute Stress Disorder
309.21   Separation Anxiety Disorder

_____ _____
_____ _____

Axis II: V71.09   No Diagnosis
799.9   Diagnosis Deferred

_____ _____
_____ _____

BALANCING WORK AND FAMILY/MULTIPLE ROLES

BEHAVIORAL DEFINITIONS

1. Experiences stress associated with balancing the multiple tasks associated with motherhood and work roles.
2. Experiences role conflict between two or more roles (i.e., obligations or responsibilities for one role interfere with ability to perform duties for other roles).
3. Describes stress and anxiety associated with cumulative demands of multiple roles.
4. Experiences fatigue and difficulty concentrating (e.g., feeling overwhelmed) due to role overload.
5. Experiences partner relationship strain and dissatisfaction due to inequitable division of responsibilities.
6. Experiences parenting relationship strain (e.g., increased conflict, low parenting efficacy, child behavioral concerns).
7. Experiences depressive and anxiety symptoms associated with workplace discrimination and limitations to occupational achievement for working mothers.
8. Demonstrates disorganization, time management concerns, and an inability to maintain commitments due to role overload.

—. _____

_____

—. _____

_____

—. _____

_____

LONG-TERM GOALS

1. Develop time management strategies to reduce role overload and role conflicts.
2. Eliminate depressive and anxiety symptoms associated with trying to balance multiple roles.
3. Develop a realistic perspective regarding demands and obligations of multiple roles and their completion.
4. Develop a support system to assist with multiple roles and responsibilities.
5. Maintain a balance between the multiple demands of motherhood, work, and other life roles and responsibilities.

—. _____

   _____

   _____

—. _____

   _____

   _____

—. _____

   _____

SHORT-TERM OBJECTIVES

1. Describe role and responsibilities associated with work and family and related thoughts, feelings, and behaviors. (1, 2)

2. Describe at least three expectations related to work and family obligations and their relationship to gender role socialization and emotional conflict. (3, 4, 5)

THERAPEUTIC INTERVENTIONS

1. Develop a supportive therapeutic relationship with the client through active listening and unconditional positive regard.

2. Explore with the client her multiple roles and responsibilities associated with work and family; clarify related thoughts and feelings.

3. Explore with the client her expectations regarding the balance between work and family, and discuss how this relates to internalized gender role stereotypes.

4. Assist the client in identifying the causes and consequences of at

least two internal and two external expectations associated with balancing work and family roles.

5. Discuss the client's potential feelings of guilt, shame, and anxiety associated with not meeting internal or external expectations.

3. Identify and replace internalized expectations and standards regarding multiple roles that are potentially harmful. (6)

6. Assist the client with identifying those expectations that are helpful and those that are potentially harmful; help the client discard those that are causing undue stress and strain and replace them with more realistic messages.

4. Clarify values and priorities. (7)

7. Help the client to explore and clarify her own values and priorities; encourage her to reduce the psychological importance placed on one or more roles to reduce the level of conflict.

5. Implement assertiveness skills and limit setting. (8)

8. Use modeling and/or role-playing to train the client in assertiveness; if indicated, refer her to an assertiveness training class/group for further instruction (see Low Self-Esteem/Lack of Assertiveness chapter in this *Planner*).

6. Research the workplace's family-friendly policies. (9)

9. Encourage the client to educate herself with regard to workplace policies (e.g., flextime, tele-commuting, job-sharing options); role-play negotiating with her boss/company to reduce role overload/conflict.

7. Learn and implement stress management and relaxation techniques to reduce fatigue, anxiety, and depressive symptoms. (10, 11)

10. Teach the client relaxation skills (e.g., progressive muscle relaxation, guided imagery, slow diaphragmatic breathing) and how to discriminate better

between relaxation and tension; teach the client how to apply these skills to her daily life (e.g., *Progressive Relaxation Training* by Bernstein and Borkovec; *Treating GAD: Evidence-Based Strategies, Tools, and Techniques* by Rygh and Sanderson).

11. Assign the client to read about progressive muscle relaxation and other calming strategies in relevant books or treatment manuals (e.g., *Progressive Relaxation Training* by Bernstein and Borkovec; *Mastery of Your Anxiety and Worry—Client Guide* by Zinbarg, Craske, Barlow, and O'Leary).

8. Communicate needs with partner regarding multiple role obligations. (12, 13, 14)

12. Refer the client to initiate conjoint therapy with partner.

13. Assist the couple in identifying conflicts that can be addressed using communication, conflict-resolution, and/or problem-solving skills (see "Behavioral Marital Therapy" by Holzworth-Munroe and Jacobson in the *Handbook of Family Therapy*, 2nd ed. by Gurman and Knickerson [Eds.]).

14. Use behavioral techniques (i.e., education, modeling, role-playing, corrective feedback, positive reinforcement) to teach communication skills, including assertive communication, offering positive feedback, active listening, making positive requests of others for behavior change, and giving negative feedback in an honest and respectful manner.

9. Learn and implement problem-solving and conflict-resolution skills. (15, 16)

15. Use behavioral techniques (i.e., education, modeling, role-playing, corrective feedback, positive reinforcement) to teach the couple problem-solving and conflict-resolution skills, including defining the problem constructively and specifically, brainstorming options, evaluating options, compromise, choosing options and implementing a plan, and evaluating the results.

16. Assign the couple a homework exercise to use and record newly learned problem-solving and conflict-resolution skills (or assign "Applying Problem-Solving to Interpersonal Conflict" in the *Adult Psychotherapy Homework Planner,* 2nd ed. by Jongsma); process results in session.

10. Protect each role from interfering with the other. (17)

17. Explore, along with the client, ways of limiting interference between multiple roles and responsibilities (e.g., when home, turn off cell phone and laptop computer; when at work, try to limit personal intrusions).

11. Identify at least five practical ways to manage stress associated with multiple demands. (18)

18. Explore, along with the client, strategies for making her life more manageable and less stressful (e.g., waking up before the children to exercise or have a cup of tea, pack the children's lunches and backpacks the night before).

12. Implement a schedule and division of home responsibilities with partner and family members. (19, 20, 21)

19. Encourage the client to develop a schedule of roles and responsibilities with her partner; assign her to meet regularly with her partner to discuss, review, and revise the schedule as needed.

20. Help the client to develop a realistic schedule that outlines the responsibilities of her partner and family members; help the client enlist the commitment of all individuals to the schedule.

21. Assign the client to conduct family meetings regularly (e.g., possibly biweekly or monthly) with children (ages 6 and up) and partner to delegate household responsibilities.

13. Identify and participate in theme support groups. (22)

22. Refer and encourage the client to join relevant support groups (e.g., single mothers, overextended women, time management).

14. Contract with three to five friends and family members who will assume active support. (23)

23. Facilitate the client's development of a social support network to assist with multiple roles and responsibilities; develop a list of active support behaviors (e.g., babysitting, help with cleaning).

15. Commit to a healthy eating, sleeping, and exercise routine. (24, 25)

24. Educate the client about, and encourage her to attend to, healthy eating, sleeping, and exercise.

25. Recommend that the client read and implement programs from *Exercising Your Way to Better Mental Health* by Leith.

16. Generate a list of self-care activities and make a commitment to regularly participate in such activities. (26)

26. Explore potential self-care activities and encourage the client's participation (or assign "Identify and Schedule Pleasant Activities" in the *Adult Psychotherapy Homework Planner,* 2nd ed. by Jongsma).

—. _____   —. _____

_____   _____

—. _____   —. _____

_____   _____

—. _____   —. _____

_____   _____

DIAGNOSTIC SUGGESTIONS:

Axis I:	309.24	Adjustment Disorder with Anxiety
	309.0	Adjustment Disorder with Depressed Mood
	309.28	Adjustment Disorder with Mixed Anxiety and Depressed Mood
	300.02	Generalized Anxiety Disorder
	300.4	Dysthymic Disorder
	_____	_____
	_____	_____

Axis II:	V71.09	No Diagnosis
	799.9	Diagnosis Deferred
	_____	_____
	_____	_____

BODY IMAGE DISTURBANCE/ EATING DISORDERS

Chapter co-authored with Karia Kelch-Oliver, MS

BEHAVIORAL DEFINITIONS

1. Demonstrates persistent preoccupation and dissatisfaction with body appearance, shape, and weight.
2. Demonstrates self-evaluation that is excessively influenced by body shape and weight.
3. Engages in persistent mirror checking, weighing, and body measuring of self.
4. Evidences increased caloric intake and rapid consumption of large amounts of food (i.e., bingeing), followed by compensatory behavior to prevent weight gain (e.g., self-induced vomiting, misuse of laxatives, diuretics, enemas, fasting, excessive exercise).
5. Demonstrates a restricted pattern of food intake and a high frequency of self-induced vomiting, misuse of laxatives, diuretics, enemas, and/or excessive exercise.
6. Evidences extreme weight loss with refusal to maintain a minimal healthy body weight.
7. Verbalizes a fear of eating and an exaggerated dread of weight gain and fat.
8. Evidences physical disturbances associated with starvation (e.g., fluid and electrolyte imbalance, cessation of menstrual periods, abdominal pain, lethargy, cold imbalance).
9. Evidences denial of being too thin and the significant medical implications of malnourished state.
10. Demonstrates a failure to recognize sensations of hunger and signs of nutritional need.
11. Exhibits a significant misperception in viewing self as too fat when emaciated and severely under recommended weight.

—. _____

_____

—. _____

_____

—. _____

_____

LONG-TERM GOALS

1. Terminate the pattern of self-starvation and restore normal eating patterns of enough nutritious foods to maintain a healthy weight.
2. Terminate the pattern of binge eating and purging behavior and return to normal eating of foods and body weight.
3. Stabilize medical conditions resulting from restricted food intake and compensatory behaviors and/or binge eating.
4. Develop an awareness of internalized unrealistic and narrow standards of women's beauty and learn to challenge such beliefs.
5. Change the definition of self to encompass positive attributes beyond body weight, size, and shape.
6. Develop effective coping strategies to deal with interpersonal stressors and emotional issues.

—. _____

_____

—. _____

_____

—. _____

_____

SHORT-TERM OBJECTIVES	THERAPEUTIC INTERVENTIONS
1. Describe eating patterns, including frequency, amounts, and types of food consumed or hoarded. (1, 2)	1. Document the client's eating pattern, including the antecedents and consequences of the eating behavior.

2. Complete psychological testing or objective questionnaires for assessing eating disorders. (3)

3. Describe any regular use of unhealthy weight control behaviors. (4, 5, 6)

4. Admit to a persistent preoccupation and dissatisfaction with body image/size. (7, 8)

2. Compare the client's eating patterns and caloric intake with an average adult rate of 1,600–2,400 calories per day to establish the reality of eating behaviors (over- or under-eating); assess the client's response to this comparison.

3. Administer to the client psychological instruments designed to objectively assess eating disorders (e.g., Eating Inventory by Stunkard and Messick, Stirling Eating Disorder Scales by Williams and Powers); give the client feedback regarding the results of the assessment.

4. Explore for the existence of vomiting behavior by the client to purge herself of caloric intake; monitor on an ongoing basis.

5. Explore the client's abuse of laxatives, diuretics, and/or enemas to control her weight; monitor on an ongoing basis.

6. Explore for a history of too vigorous and too frequent exercise by the client in an effort to control her weight; monitor on an ongoing basis.

7. Provide the client with an overview of body image disturbance and/or disordered eating including basic information, psychological and physical complications, and myths/magic numbers (e.g., a certain dress size or number on the scale is "good" and another "bad").

8. Explore the client's level of preoccupation/dissatisfaction with eating, weight, and body

image to determine if the preoccupation is causing significant distress or significantly interferes with functioning.

5. Participate in a complete physical exam and dental exam. (9)

9. Refer the client to a physician for a physical exam and maintain close consultation with the physician regarding the client's medical condition and nutritional habits; refer the client to a dentist for an evaluation to determine if frequent vomiting may have damaged her teeth.

6. Cooperate with admission to inpatient treatment if one's medical condition necessitates such treatment. (10)

10. Refer the client for hospitalization, as necessary, if her weight loss becomes severe in order to restore weight and to address fluid and electrolyte imbalances.

7. Keep a journal of daily incidents of behaviors demonstrating body image preoccupation. (11, 12)

11. Assign the client to keep a journal of mirror checking (or avoiding looking in the mirror), body measuring, and/or efforts to camouflage her body.

12. Review the client's journal material, processing the preoccupation with a distorted body image and confronting denial, minimization, or rationalization.

8. Eat at regular intervals, consuming at least the minimum daily calories necessary to progressively gain weight and terminate the pattern of starvation or overeating. (13, 14)

13. Refer the client to a nutritionist or assist the client in establishing a balanced daily diet of a specific calorie total; solicit written agreement to follow this diet.

14. Provide the client with positive reinforcement for weight gain rather than for eating behavior.

9. Identify and change distorted self-talk messages associated with eating behavior. (15, 16)

15. Provide the client's with nutrition-related references and educational materials.

16. Challenge the client's irrational food and weight myths (e.g., "carbohydrates are fattening" and "to be avoided," "fluid intake results in weight gain"); teach her to establish realistic messages regarding food and body weight.

10. Verbalize a more positive body image that is disconnected from rigid/narrow sociocultural messages. (17, 18)

17. Educate the client on the relationship between sociocultural messages regarding women's beauty (e.g., emphasis on thinness as a requirement for attractiveness) and her body image.

18. Reinforce positive affirmations, imagery, mirror work, drawing or sculpting one's body, and provide feedback to help correct body image distortions.

11. Implement three new healthy and appropriate strategies to cope with stress, depression, and anxiety rather than using unhealthy eating patterns. (3, 19, 20, 21)

3. Administer to the client psychological instruments designed to objectively assess eating disorders (e.g., Eating Inventory by Stunkard and Messick, Stirling Eating Disorder Scales by Williams and Powers); give the client feedback regarding the results of the assessment.

19. Assist the client in identifying cues that lead to unhealthy eating by assigning her to write a daily journal of eating behavior, thoughts, and feelings.

20. Assist the client in developing more adaptive strategies and behaviors (e.g., relaxation, read a book, call a friend) to cope with uncomfortable emotional states.

21. Assist the client in preparing to cope with future depressive or anxious symptoms and monitoring feelings in order to prevent

relapses (e.g., prevent relapse by learning to recognize, respect, and respond to internal bodily cues such as feeling tired, anxious) and recognizing situations that trigger urges to binge, starve, or otherwise abuse food and plan other activities (e.g., engage in a favorite hobby such as listening to music, reading).

12. Verbalize a definition of self that includes qualities beyond body weight, size, and shape. (22, 23, 24, 25)

22. Challenge the client's basis for construing herself in terms of shape so the concept of self goes beyond body weight; help her define herself in terms of relationships with family, friends, and spirituality, and in terms of accomplishments, traits, and abilities.

23. Challenge the client to develop her strengths, talent, and intelligence and not hide these qualities to protect others' ego.

24. Assist the client in developing internal standards of approval and reduce the need for external approval by brainstorming her positive attributes and qualities (e.g., personality, values, behavior).

25. Encourage the client to develop competencies in other areas of life (e.g., sports, hobbies, educational activities) to increase feelings of self-worth and self-esteem.

13. Increase the number of realistic, positive messages regarding eating, food, and body size to at least three per day. (26, 27)

26. Assist the client in identifying her self-defeating thoughts regarding food, eating, and body size (e.g., overgeneralizing and all-or-nothing thinking); help her replace these distortions with

more realistic, positive cognitions.

27. Assign the client to write three positive messages per day regarding food, eating, and body image; monitor her compliance, reinforcing for success and redirecting for failure.

14. Verbalize acceptance of control, self-determination, and responsibility for one's body image and eating behavior. (28)

28. Instill hope and the taking of responsibility for one's actions (including setbacks) into the client's perceptions of socio-cultural pressures regarding body image, eating, and treatment; view setbacks as opportunities to learn more about eating habits and to reduce the guilt that sets the stage for longer relapses.

15. Identify and strengthen ties to people and circumstances that affirm self-worth. (29)

29. Encourage the client to seek out situations, jobs, and people that affirm her self-worth and avoid situations or people that are harmful or demeaning; assist her in identifying affirming versus demeaning people and circumstances.

16. Family members and/or partner verbalize an understanding of the need to refrain from responsibility for the client's eating behavior. (30, 31, 32)

30. Educate the client's parents or partner to detach from taking responsibility for the client's eating behavior without be-coming indifferent or hostile.

31. Discuss with the client's parents or partner effective relationships that include both nurturing and privacy/autonomy.

32. Encourage the client's family members to read material on eating disorders (e.g., *Surviving an Eating Disorder: Strategies for Families and Friends* by Siegel, Brisman, and Weinshel;

17. Attend a body image/eating disorders support group. (33, 34)

18. Engage in social and/or educational activities that connect personal and social change. (35)

19. Complete a readministration of objective tests of eating disorders and reevaluate her preoccupation/ dissatisfaction with body via discussion as a means of assessing treatment outcome. (8, 36)

20. Complete a survey to assess the degree of satisfaction with treatment. (37)

Eating Disorders by National Institute of Mental Health).

33. Refer the client to a support group for eating disorders.

34. Monitor the client's attendance at an eating disorders group; process the experience and support valuable insights gained.

35. Refer the client to educational sessions or activity groups that promote body image acceptance (e.g. sponsoring a letter-writing campaign directed toward advertisers outlining offensive or destructive, as well as positive messages).

8. Explore the client's level of preoccupation/dissatisfaction with eating, weight, and body image to determine if the pre-occupation is causing significant distress or significantly interferes with functioning.

36. Assess the outcome of treatment by readministering to the client objective tests of eating disorders; evaluate the results and provide feedback to the client.

37. Administer a survey to assess the client's degree of satisfaction with treatment.

—. _____

_____

—. _____

_____

—. _____

_____

—. _____

_____

—. _____

_____

—. _____

_____

DIAGNOSTIC SUGGESTIONS:

Axis I: 307.1   Anorexia Nervosa
          307.51   Bulimia Nervosa
          307.50   Eating Disorder NOS

          _____   _____

          _____   _____

Axis II: 301.4   Obsessive-Compulsive Personality Disorder
          V71.09   No Diagnosis
          799.9   Diagnosis Deferred

          _____   _____

          _____   _____

CAREER SUCCESS OBSTACLES

BEHAVIORAL DEFINITIONS

1. Verbalizes low career expectations and aspirations due to restricted self-concept.
2. Experiences employment dissatisfaction due to limited or no recognition/credit for work efforts or product.
3. Verbalizes feelings of being underutilized or overlooked at work due to inequitable allocation of work projects, including not being assigned challenging or rewarding projects.
4. Experiences frustration or disappointment due to continually being overlooked for promotions.
5. Verbalizes feelings of powerlessness or hopelessness due to inequitable salary differentials.
6. Experiences isolation due to exclusion from or restricted access to informal social networks, typically available to male colleagues, in which business transactions are discussed and executed.
7. Feels "lost" or disoriented due to lack of mentoring opportunities or access to role models, particularly in male-dominated occupations.
8. Experiences anxiety, hopelessness, and distress due to sexual harassment or other hostile/degrading behaviors in the work environment.
9. Experiences distress and role overload due to a work environment that limits the ability to integrate family responsibilities with career advancement.
10. Verbalizes fear of maintaining employment or low career fulfillment due to the lack of job performance feedback during evaluation periods.

—. _____

_____

—. _____

_____

—. _____

_____

LONG-TERM GOALS

1. Explore career options that have been automatically ruled out due to low self-concept or limited opportunities.
2. Develop assertiveness skills and techniques for application in work-related activities (e.g., establishing boundaries with coworkers, negotiating salary).
3. Develop skills to counteract sex-role stereotypes and the elements of the work environment that have negatively impacted self-esteem.
4. Engage in mentoring or role-model programs designed to facilitate career advancement.
5. Learn and implement various coping skills for dealing with work- and career-related inequalities.
6. Develop advocacy and empowerment skills that involve taking a proactive stance in the work environment.

—. _____

_____

—. _____

_____

—. _____

_____

SHORT-TERM OBJECTIVES

1. Verbalize feelings of distress and dissatisfaction related to obstacles to career success. (1, 2)

THERAPEUTIC INTERVENTIONS

1. Explore the client's perception of her career success obstacles, including both overt and covert discriminatory practices related to gender, race/ethnicity, religion, and sexual orientation.

2. Validate the client's experience and explore how the work environment impacts distress and

dissatisfaction; assist her in listing the three most frustrating aspects of her employment.

2. Identify three work situations that contribute to depression, anxiety, and stress. (2)

2. Validate the client's experience and explore how the work environment impacts distress and dissatisfaction; assist her in listing the three most frustrating aspects of her employment.

3. Identify work/career-related racism, sexism, and discrimination (e.g., experience of tokenism, stereotyping). (3)

3. Assist the client in recognizing discriminatory aspects of the work environment.

4. Implement effective problem-solving skills to deal with a discriminatory work environment. (4)

4. Teach the client effective problem-solving skills (e.g., clarify the problem, brainstorm solutions, consult with others for additional solutions, list the pros and cons of each solution, select and implement a plan of action, evaluate the consequences, redirect efforts if necessary) to deal with those aspects of the work environment that limit career development and participation.

5. Identify and replace at least three negative self-talk statements that perpetuate feelings of powerlessness or hopelessness. (5, 6)

5. Assist the client in identifying negative, career-related, self-talk statements and specific situations that serve as triggers.

6. Assist the client in reframing her negative self-talk while still validating the experience of barriers and obstacles.

6. Explore and identify three ways in which one's socialization process has affected career choices or is contributing to career obstacles. (7, 8)

7. Explore gender-role messages the client received while growing up regarding career options and behaviors (e.g., girls are not to be assertive; girls should defer careers to household responsibilities).

7. Identify and replace cognitive self-talk that contributes to all-or-nothing thinking, gender-role stereotypes, or low career self-efficacy. (9, 10, 11)

8. Explore the extent to which the client has internalized these gender role messages and how they impact her career aspirations and work behaviors (e.g., interactions with coworkers, delegation of tasks, negotiating salary, confronting obstacles).

9. Assist the client in developing an awareness of her internalized cognitive messages that may limit career success (e.g., "I cannot be a mother and have a career"; "Women do not belong in scientific occupations").

10. Assign the client to keep a daily journal of experiences, automatic negative thoughts associated with experiences, and the resulting restricted behavior; process the journal material to diffuse destructive thinking patterns and replace them with alternative positive thoughts.

11. Reinforce the client's positive, realistic cognitive messages that enhance self-confidence and increase proactive career pursuits.

8. Read materials related to women who have attained career success. (12)

12. Assign the client to read books such as *Mentoring Heroes: 52 Fabulous Women's Paths to Success and the Mentors Who Empowered Them* by Doyle and *Power Tools for Women: Plugging into the Essential Skills for Work and Life* by Daniels; process the content.

9. Participate in mentoring/role-modeling programs designed to increase career self-efficacy. (13)

13. Refer the client to shadowing or mentorship programs/workshops for aspiring career women.

10. Obtain support from other career women and learn strategies for success in the face of obstacles. (14)

11. Develop standards of achievement and approval as a basis for an internal locus of evaluation in order to minimize self-blame and increase confidence. (15)

12. Implement relaxation and meditation techniques to manage and process career frustrations. (16)

13. Increase self-esteem and self-concept by exploring and encompassing other roles/identities besides those of career. (17, 18)

14. Develop career-related strategies to overcome and persist in the face of obstacles. (19, 20, 21)

14. Refer the client to educational seminars, informational meetings, and other related activities to meet other career women and learn career success strategies.

15. Assist the client in decreasing external locus of evaluation (e.g., coworkers, supervisors, peers) and develop her own standards of achievement and approval.

16. Train the client in relaxation (e.g., deep muscle, deep breathing, guided imagery) and/or meditation techniques; encourage implementation of stress-reduction procedures.

17. Explore how career accomplishments and frustrations have become incorporated into the client's self-evaluation.

18. Reality-test or explore non-career-related accomplishments or abilities that can be incorporated into the client's self-evaluation and overall self-concept.

19. Facilitate role-play and behavioral rehearsal with the client focused on developing career success strategies and skills (e.g., negotiating salary, handling sexual harassment, developing assertiveness skills); discuss potential implications (positive and negative) of implementing such strategies.

20. Encourage the client to develop newly acquired skills further by reality-testing them in work situations; review the attempts at implementation, reinforcing

success and redirecting for failure.

21. Assign the client to read *Seven Secrets of Successful Women: Strategies of the Women Who've Made It* by Brooks and Brooks; process the content.

15. Identify barriers and personal benefits to balancing career and family life. (22, 23)

22. Explore the client's perception of her personal benefits of combining career and family.

23. Explore the client's perception of existing and potential barriers and obstacles.

16. Identify options for assistance with family responsibilities. (24)

24. Assist the client in identifying options for assistance with family responsibilities, (e.g., day care, respite care, increased delegation to spouse and/or children).

17. Discuss with the family the need for assistance with responsibilities at home. (25)

25. Conduct a family session that focuses on the client negotiating and reassigning home-related roles and responsibilities among family members.

18. Participate in or advocate for benefits and services in the workplace environment that foster career/family balance. (26)

26. Explore advocacy measures that the client could pursue to increase employer awareness of benefits and services needed to support family/career balance and connection.

19. Identify three methods of developing support systems outside of work to provide validation and encouragement and increase coping effectiveness. (27)

27. Explore with the client her available positive support system outside of work and discuss ways to develop this further, if needed.

—. _____

_____

—. _____

_____

—. _____

_____

—. _____

_____

—. _____   —. _____

_____   _____

DIAGNOSTIC SUGGESTIONS:

Axis I:	309.24	Adjustment Disorder with Anxiety
	309.0	Adjustment Disorder with Depressed Mood
	309.28	Adjustment Disorder with Mixed Anxiety and Depressed Mood
	V62.2	Occupational Problem
	296.xx	Major Depressive Disorder
	300.00	Anxiety Disorder NOS

_____   _____

_____   _____

Axis II:	V71.09	No Diagnosis
	799.9	Diagnosis Deferred

_____   _____

_____   _____

CAREGIVING OF AGING PARENTS

Chapter co-authored with Wendi S. Williams, PhD

BEHAVIORAL DEFINITIONS

1. Exhibits anxiety and grief related to change in parent-child dynamics due to assuming caregiving responsibilities for parents.
2. Experiences stress and frustration associated with caregiving responsibilities.
3. Experiences psychological distress associated with "unfinished business" as it relates to aging parent(s) (e.g., parent-child conflict, sibling relationships, familial role expectations).
4. Describes strain in sibling relationships related to disproportional involvement in parental caregiving responsibilities.
5. Describes strain in relationship with partner/spouse related to parental caregiving responsibilities.
6. Demonstrates difficulty managing caregiving with existing roles and responsibilities (i.e., home, family, and work).

—. _____
_____
—. _____
_____
_____
—. _____
_____

LONG-TERM GOALS

1. Resolve associated grief and anxiety and adapt to new caregiving role and life circumstances.
2. Develop perception of parental caregiving as an opportunity for psychological and personal growth; acknowledge the benefits and the challenges.

3. Develop a balance between caregiving responsibilities and other roles, responsibilities, and interests.
4. Resolve psychological distress related to family systems dynamics; resolve strain in relationship with partner(s) and other family members.
5. Develop a social support network for self and aging parent(s).

—. _____

_____

—. _____

_____

—. _____

_____

SHORT-TERM OBJECTIVES

1. Describe family history and details of current caretaking situation. (1, 2, 3)

2. Verbalize an understanding of the physical, psychological, behavioral, and spiritual impact of aging and the related complications on parent(s). (4, 5)

THERAPEUTIC INTERVENTIONS

1. Cultivate a safe, trusting therapeutic environment through verbal and nonverbal displays of unconditional positive regard, warmth, empathy, and acceptance.

2. Document the client's family history, including age, health, and relationship dynamics of her parent(s), sibling(s), child(ren), and partner(s).

3. Explore the details of the client's caregiving duties for her parents.

4. Educate the client on the process of aging, its impact on the life of the parent(s) (e.g., potential loss and grief reactions), and the related increased needs and limitations.

5. Educate the client on the impact of degenerative diseases and conditions (e.g., Alzheimer's) on

the psychological functioning and activities of daily living for aging parent(s).

3. Verbalize a comprehension of the type and schedule of prescribed medications, potential side effects, and other treatment regimens of parent(s). (6)

6. Refer the client to a physician to gain a greater understanding of her parent(s)' medication regimen and its expected effectiveness and/or side effects.

4. Describe thoughts and feelings associated with the transition to parental caregiving. (7, 8, 9)

7. Explore recent adjustments to the client's life given her new caregiving role; assign journaling homework to explore related thoughts and feelings.

8. Explore the aspects of parental aging that are contributing to the client's stress and anxiety.

9. Process the client's mourning, regarding the loss of her previous parent-child relationship and her adjustment to new relationship dynamics and expectations.

5. Access informational resources on parental caregiving. (10)

10. Refer the client to resources on caring for aging/ill parents (e.g., books, Internet, interviewing other caregivers); discuss and process this information.

6. Describe family values and sociocultural expectations regarding the responsibility of adult children to aging/ill parents. (11)

11. Explore, along with the client, familial and sociocultural messages regarding caregiving responsibilities for aging/ill parent(s), women's traditional roles as caregivers, and their impact on the client.

7. Identify at least three benefits and challenges of parental caregiving responsibilities. (12)

12. Explore, along with the client, the benefits and challenges of assuming parental caretaking responsibilities; begin to generate ideas regarding approaches and resources to help minimize difficulties.

8. Identify parent-child relationship dynamics (i.e., unfinished family business) that complicate care for aging parent. (13, 14)

13. Explore the client's relationship history with aging/ill parent(s) and process unresolved issues; examine options (e.g., group counseling, process issues directly with parent, process issues with siblings) for handling emotional dynamics and implications.

14. Process the client's regression to earlier stages of development and corresponding emotional and behavioral manifestations.

9. Develop effective communication skills and boundaries that will facilitate a harmonious relationship and caregiving of aging parent. (15, 16)

15. Participate in role-playing and modeling experiential exercises with the client in order to facilitate effective communication with her parent(s).

16. Practice communication with the client in ways that will honor parental autonomy and decision-making regarding care while maintaining limits and boundaries.

10. Identify at least two internal and two external resources that will reduce stress and isolation related to parental caregiving. (17)

17. Explore the client's internal strengths (e.g., insight, coping strategies) and external resources (e.g., friends, religious institutions) that will assist with parental caregiving; refer the client to appropriate community services.

11. Increase social support contacts to reduce isolation and stress related to new role expectations. (18, 19, 20)

18. Explore the client's current support network and coping strategies as she tries to adjust to the current life stress related to providing care for her adult parent(s); assist in identifying options to overcome isolation related to new role responsibilities.

12. Identify and replace distorted, unrealistic self-talk regarding caring for aging parents that triggers negative emotions. (21, 22, 23, 24)

19. Refer the client to a support group of adult children of aging parents.

20. Encourage the client to maintain contact with friends and other family members, sharing feelings generated by the parental caregiving.

21. Assist the client in developing an awareness of automatic thoughts that reflect unrealistic expectations regarding caring for aging parents.

22. Assign the client to keep a daily journal of dysfunctional automatic thoughts associated with caring for aging parents (e.g., "Negative Thoughts Trigger Negative Feelings" in the *Adult Psychotherapy Homework Planner,* 2nd ed. by Jongsma; "Daily Record of Dysfunctional Thoughts" in *Cognitive Therapy of Depression* by Beck, Rush, Shaw, and Emery); process the journal material to challenge unrealistic thinking patterns and replace them with reality-based thoughts.

23. Do "behavioral experiments" in which unrealistic automatic thoughts are treated as hypotheses/predictions, reality-based alternative hypotheses/predictions are generated, and both are tested against the client's past, present, and/or future experiences.

24. Reinforce the client's positive, reality-based cognitive messages that enhance self-confidence and increase adaptive action (see

"Positive Self-Talk" in the *Adult Psychotherapy Homework Planner,* 2nd ed. by Jongsma).

13. Increase communication with siblings and significant others to elicit support and assistance with caregiving responsibilities. (25, 26, 27)

25. Explore the client's historical familial relationships and their influence on current family relations that impact the caregiving relationship.

26. Role-play with the client negotiating and managing the roles and responsibilities of caring for aging/ill parent(s) with significant others.

27. Facilitate family-therapy sessions to elicit support from significant others and provide opportunities for the family to address caregiving responsibilities cooperatively.

14. Develop time management strategies that allow for balanced accommodation of new role responsibilities. (28, 29)

28. Explore the impact of caregiving responsibilities on the client's ability to manage multiple roles and responsibilities.

29. Assist the client with generating a realistic and effective time management schedule.

15. Implement stress management practices aimed at a restoration of physical and emotional balance. (30, 31)

30. Assist the client in developing a list of enjoyable activities that will assist with stress reduction (or assign "Identify and Schedule Pleasant Activities" in the *Adult Psychotherapy Homework Planner,* 2nd ed. by Jongsma).

31. Assist the client in identifying areas of daily living (e.g., nutrition, exercise, sleep, spirituality) that need modification to reduce stress.

16. Identify coping strategies to effectively process inevitable loss of parent(s). (32)

32. Assist the client with addressing grief and mourning issues related to the loss of her parent; educate

	the client on the process of grief and potential reactions.
17. Develop awareness and acceptance of one's own aging process. (33)	33. Discuss with the client her feelings/reactions regarding her own aging and related implications.

__. _____   __. _____

_____   _____

__. _____   __. _____

_____   _____

__. _____   __. _____

_____   _____

DIAGNOSTIC SUGGESTIONS:

Axis I:

309.24	Adjustment Disorder with Anxiety
309.0	Adjustment Disorder with Depressed Mood
309.28	Adjustment Disorder with Mixed Anxiety and Depressed Mood
308.3	Acute Stress Disorder
300.02	Generalized Anxiety Disorder
296.2x	Major Depressive Disorder, Single Episode
V62.82	Bereavement

_____ _____

_____ _____

Axis II:

V71.09	No Diagnosis
799.9	Diagnosis Deferred

_____ _____

_____ _____

CHEMICAL DEPENDENCE

Chapter co-authored with Telsie A. Davis, EdS

BEHAVIORAL DEFINITIONS

1. Consistently uses mood-altering substance(s) in greater amounts and over a longer period of time than intended.
2. Demonstrates increased tolerance of a substance so that more is needed to produce the desired effect.
3. Continues use of a substance despite persistent or recurring physical, legal, vocational, or social problems that are directly caused by the use of the substance.
4. Demonstrates a large time investment in searching for and obtaining mood-altering substances, and recovering from their effects.
5. Denies that substance use is a problem despite feedback from family, loved ones, friends, coworkers, and/or employer that substance use is out of control and negatively affecting her.
6. Verbalizes feelings of depression, anxiety, shame, and/or powerlessness over the inability to stop or reduce the use of mood-altering substances.
7. Minimizes the severity of substance use due to fear of reprisal, punishment, and/or loss of custody of children.
8. Reports physical symptoms (e.g., muscle aches, shaking, seizures, nausea, flu-like symptoms, depression, anxiety, irritability) when use of the substance is discontinued.
9. Spends increased amounts of time using mood-altering substances in isolation and in secret.
10. Verbalizes a diminished sense of self-worth due to behaviors (e.g., lying, stealing, promiscuity) committed while obtaining or under the influence of mood-altering substances.
11. Plans the time and length of activities (e.g., errands, family outings, social events, vacations) around the amount of substances held in possession or the ability to obtain substances.
12. Cancels or reschedules important social or occupational activities because they interfere with using substances or occur while intoxicated or high.

—. _____
_____
—. _____
_____
—. _____
_____

LONG-TERM GOALS

1. Acknowledge chemical dependence and understand its biological, psychological, and social effects on self, children, family, and friends.
2. Actively participate in a sustained recovery program, living a lifestyle free from the use of mood-altering substances.
3. Learn and implement skills to effectively cope with anxiety, depression, relapse triggers, and life stressors.
4. Create a living environment that supports a healthy physical, psychological, and spiritual lifestyle.
5. Develop increased self-esteem through awareness of personal strengths and achievements.
6. Develop a sober and empowered identity by resolving (or reducing) thoughts and feelings of powerlessness, worthlessness, guilt, shame, and self-blame.

—. _____
_____
—. _____
_____
—. _____
_____

SHORT-TERM OBJECTIVES

1. Describe substance abuse history, including route, amount, and pattern of use. (1, 2, 3)

THERAPEUTIC INTERVENTIONS

1. Create a therapeutic environment of trust, safety, and respect through verbal and nonverbal displays of unconditional positive regard, empathy, and acceptance.

2. Gather a complete substance abuse history (e.g., route, amount, and pattern of use; consequences experienced as a result of substance abuse); assess for history of physical and/or sexual abuse victimization associated with the client's substance abuse.

3. Validate the client's experience and affirm that she has the capacity to improve her life.

2. Obtain a medical examination to evaluate the physiological effects of chemical dependence and need for any medical treatment. (4, 5)

4. Refer the client for a thorough medical exam to determine any physical effects of chemical dependence and the need for medical treatment.

5. Educate the client about the importance of treatment and medication compliance, if needed, and reinforce compliance as a self-care behavior.

3. Participate in recommended mental health assessments to identify any co-occurring disorders. (6)

6. Refer the client for or perform a thorough psychological exam to determine the presence of any co-occurring disorders and the need for supportive therapy and treatment; be mindful that painful memories associated with physical and/or sexual abuse victimization may reoccur once sober or increase the likelihood of relapse.

4. Take all medications as prescribed and report any side effects to the therapist and/or physician. (7)

7. Refer the client to a physician for a medication assessment.

5. Verbalize an understanding of chemical dependence and identify negative biological, psychological, and social consequences of addiction. (8, 9)

8. Educate the client about the cycle of chemical dependence and the consequences of addiction (e.g., risk of developing liver disease, hypoglycemia and diabetes, fertility problems, and perinatal

mortality and morbidity if pregnant).

9. Facilitate an awareness of the negative social consequences experienced as a result of chemical dependency (e.g., sexual risk-taking, financial cost, possible removal of children by legal authorities); process related thoughts and feelings.

6. Acknowledge the social stigma deterrent to acknowledging chemical dependence to friends and family. (10)

10. Discuss with the client the relationship between gender, the stigma associated with drug use, and her reluctance to seek help from friends and family, especially if she is pregnant or has children.

7. Decrease denial of addiction as evidenced by making statements reflecting the true severity of substance use and its negative impact on all aspects of life. (11, 12, 13)

11. Assign the client to interview three loved ones to obtain an understanding of the severity of her addiction, and to learn how her addiction negatively impacts others.

12. Identify and process the client's denial strategies (e.g., avoidance and rationalizing) that minimize the severity of substance use and disrupt her progress in recovery.

13. Engage the client in Motivational Enhancement Therapy (e.g., reflective listening, person-centered interviewing) when she has been identified as being in a stage of change where any resistance or ambivalence exists (e.g., precontemplation, contemplation, or preparation); educate her about the benefits of professional help.

8. Make verbal "I statements" that reflect acceptance of chemical dependence and the need and desire for help. (14, 15, 16)

14. Positively reinforce statements that reflect acceptance of chemical dependency, its destructive consequences for self and others, and the need for help.

15. Explore and normalize fears and reluctance to commit to sobriety while assuring the client of her capacity to successfully recover.

16. Assist the client in identifying and processing the potential benefits of sobriety.

9. Verbalize insights gained from groups, reading literature, and talking with women who are successfully recovering from chemical dependence. (17)

17. Assign the client to read literature specifically for women in recovery (e.g., *The Fight Within: A Story of Women in Recovery* by Miller) and attend AA lectures and/or psychoeducational groups about chemical dependence.

10. Reduce secrecy and increase accountability by confiding chemical dependency and commitment to recovery to a minimum of two supportive persons. (18)

18. Assist the client in identifying at least two supportive persons in whom she can confide and by whom she can be held accountable regarding chemical dependence recovery efforts.

11. Write a good-bye letter to substance(s) of choice. (19)

19. Assign the client to write a good-bye letter to substance(s) of choice as if it were a person, detailing the progression of the relationship and reasons why it will no longer be a part of her life; review and process the letter in session.

12. Develop a written relapse prevention plan to support long-term abstinence. (20)

20. Educate the client about relapse and assist her in developing a personal relapse prevention plan to support long-term abstinence.

13. Identify the reasons for substance use and learn healthy coping methods. (21, 22)

21. Explore how the client uses substance abuse as an escape from stress, physical and emotional pain, and/or boredom.

22. Educate the client about personality, social, and family factors that foster her chemical dependence and explore healthy ways to get her needs met.

14. Develop a list of all people, places, and/or situations (triggers) that increase the likelihood of substance use; learn two strategies to successfully cope with each trigger. (23, 24, 25)

23. Assist the client in identifying personal, interpersonal, environmental, and situational triggers that increase her likelihood of using mood-altering substances; be mindful of crises associated with chemical dependence in women (e.g., miscarriage, divorce, unemployment, recent departure of a child from home).

24. Teach the client about, and role-play with her, coping and drug-refusal strategies (e.g., using positive affirmations, journaling, taking a daily inventory and saying "no" to using mood-altering substances) in order to increase healthy coping mechanisms.

25. Facilitate identification of strategies that the client has used successfully in the past to cope with triggers; encourage and reinforce their current implementation.

15. Identify, challenge, and replace destructive self-talk with positive, strength-building self-talk. (26, 27)

26. Explore the client's schema and self-talk that weaken her resolve to remain abstinent; challenge the biases; assist her in generating realistic self-talk that correct for the biases and build resilience.

27. Rehearse situations in which the client identifies her negative self-talk and generates empowering alternatives (or assign "Negative Thoughts Trigger Negative Feelings" in the *Adult Psychotherapy Homework Planner,* 2nd ed. by Jongsma); review and reinforce success.

16. Assess friendships and intimate relationships to identify any changes needed to make personal life conducive to recovery. (28)

28. Educate the client about, and process with her, characteristics of a healthy adult relationship; assess the healthiness and satisfaction of her current relationships.

17. Build positive relationships with at least three women to form a sober support system and keep their names and contact numbers on an emergency card to be carried at all times. (29)

29. Help the client identify places to meet women in recovery (e.g., AA) and encourage the client to ask for their support; assign the client to keep names and contact numbers of supportive persons with her at all times.

18. Identify and become involved in fun, sober, recreational, and social activities that will replace substance abuse-related activities. (30)

30. Brainstorm with the client enjoyable, sober social gatherings and recreational activities.

19. Replace addictions with new lifestyles that include school, work, community service, and physical activity. (31)

31. Assist the client in replacing addiction behaviors with new lifestyles by exploring opportunities to be involved in school, work, and/or community activities.

20. Learn and practice effective parenting strategies. (32)

32. Teach the client how to develop, and role-play with her, strategies for effective communication, creating healthy family rules, maintaining the parent role, and being an active parent.

21. Practice identifying and correcting negative and/or false beliefs and self-talk. (33, 34, 35)

33. Confront self-disparaging or false statements and beliefs (e.g., "I don't deserve to be happy because

of the pain I have caused my family").

34. Teach the client about, and model for her, cognitive restructuring to help her identify, dispute, and correct negative or false beliefs and self-talk; reframe messages to increase internalized positive messages about self.

35. Affirm and facilitate the client's awareness of her personal strengths, talents, and potential.

22. Develop and implement a self-care plan that supports optimal functioning in all areas of life. (36)

36. Assist the client in developing a self-care plan that involves nurturing every aspect of her life including physical, psychological, social, and/or spiritual components; encourage and positively reinforce implementation of self-nurturing behaviors.

23. Identify three job opportunities that would provide financial stability; explore ways of obtaining the necessary education and training. (37)

37. Engage the client in career counseling to explore job opportunities and related education and training needed.

24. Make and distribute an invitation inviting loved ones to a family education session with the therapist. (38)

38. Facilitate a family session with the client and her loved one(s), teaching about and discussing the cycle of addiction and the process of recovery in order to bolster support, reinforce gains made, and facilitate relapse prevention.

—. _____   —. _____

_____   _____

—. _____   —. _____

_____   _____

—. _____   —. _____

_____   _____

DIAGNOSTIC SUGGESTIONS:

Axis I:	303.90	Alcohol Dependence
	305.0	Alcohol Abuse
	304.40	Amphetamine Dependence
	305.70	Amphetamine Abuse
	304.30	Cannabis Dependence
	304.20	Cocaine Dependence
	305.60	Cocaine Abuse
	304.80	Polysubstance Dependence
	304.10	Sedative, Hypnotic, or Anxiolytic Dependence
	_____	_____
	_____	_____

Axis II:	V71.09	No Diagnosis
	799.9	Diagnosis Deferred
	_____	_____
	_____	_____

CHILDBEARING/REARING DECISIONS

BEHAVIORAL DEFINITIONS

1. Struggles with the decision whether and/or when to have (or forego) children based on issues such as infertility, career advancement, financial resources, personal values, and religious beliefs.
2. Experiences conflict with partner regarding reproductive plans and the decision to have a child or children.
3. Struggles with the change in childbearing/rearing plans as a result of life experiences, attitude changes, or change in living conditions, finances, and/or ability to have/raise children.
4. Experiences stress related to difficulty or inability to plan the number and timing of children due to factors such as unplanned pregnancies or contraception failure.
5. Experiences internal and external pressure from friends, family, and peers to have children.
6. Struggles with the decision whether or not to bear, adopt, or raise children as a single mother.

__. _____

_____

__. _____

_____

__. _____

_____

LONG-TERM GOALS

1. Develop an effective decision-making approach to address whether and when to bear/raise children.
2. Resolve the issue of whether to have children through natural childbirth, adoption, or single parenting.
3. Resolve conflict with partner regarding reproductive goals and the decision to have children.
4. Develop an informed and flexible plan regarding childbearing/rearing with consideration to other life roles and demands (e.g., work, career, education).
5. Resolve the stressors associated with the incompatibility between childbearing/rearing goals, life experiences, attitude changes, living conditions, finances, and/or ability to conceive children.

—. _____

_____

—. _____

_____

—. _____

_____

SHORT-TERM OBJECTIVES	THERAPEUTIC INTERVENTIONS
1. Verbalize thoughts and feelings regarding childbearing in a safe therapeutic setting. (1, 2, 3)	1. Provide a nonjudgmental stance that fosters honest self-disclosure regarding attitudes toward childbearing plans.
	2. Assist the client in exploring the advantages and disadvantages of having children or not and how many.
	3. Assist the client in drafting an outline of childbearing goals.
2. Verbalize anxieties related to childbearing decisions. (4)	4. Explore the client's anxieties and fears; validate her stress response.

3. Describe the internal and external pressures associated with childbearing decisions. (5, 6)

5. Explore with the client the gender-role messages that she received from family and society about childbearing; explore the extent to which the client internalized such messages.

6. Reinforce the client's personal wants and needs with regard to childbearing.

4. Articulate the perceptions of motherhood and their relationship to decision making. (7)

7. Explore the client's images of motherhood and the degree to which she believes she meets these ideals; discuss discrepancies between realistic and ideal images and resultant anxieties.

5. Replace unrealistic expectations regarding motherhood with more realistic and healthy ones. (8)

8. Assist the client with exploring and challenging unrealistic perceptions and fears related to being the "perfect" mother.

6. Implement at least four positive ways of coping with childbearing/rearing stressors. (9, 10)

9. Explore the approaches the client has used to cope with stressors; identify both positive and negative aspects of these approaches.

10. Assist the client in replacing negative/counterproductive coping strategies with positive/productive coping strategies; encourage those that lead to psychological and physical well-being (e.g., replace smoking with exercising).

7. Verbalize and reframe negative self-talk about childbearing decisions. (11, 12)

11. Reframe the client's negative self-talk (e.g., "I can't get pregnant because I am being punished for being a bad person"; "Having children will diminish my attractiveness") and assist her in establishing more realistic messages about childbearing decision making.

8. Identify ways to increase the likelihood of the desired childbearing outcome occurring. (13, 14)

9. Acknowledge having limited control over childbearing plans. (15, 16)

10. Identify any conflicts in roles and demands and identify at least three possible solutions to these conflicts. (17, 18, 19)

11. Develop a support system of individuals who are

12. Assign the client to repeat to herself two positive messages per day about her childbearing decision.

13. Assist the client in identifying her desired solutions to the childbearing issue.

14. Assist the client in describing the types of resources and supports available to her to achieve a desired outcome to her childbearing dilemma.

15. Explore expectations with the client regarding childbearing plans; validate the potential disappointment associated with unmet expectations.

16. Explore ways of finding satisfaction with life's unexpectedness (e.g., increased participation in activities that are fulfilling).

17. Assist the client in identifying role conflict or overload (e.g., being a student and having parenting responsibilities).

18. Explore with the client possible solutions to role conflict and overload (e.g., postpone having children; speak with boss/employer about flextime, time off, job sharing; hire a babysitter to assist with childcare so that she can complete school assignments).

19. Refer the client to programs (e.g., childcare centers) that offer assistance and provide support as needed.

20. Assess the client's current level of social support.

experiencing or have experienced similar difficulties. (20, 21)

12. Communicate needs with partner regarding multiple role obligations. (22, 23)

13. Identify at least two core themes related to conflict with partner regarding childbearing/rearing issue and overtly communicate about them. (24, 25)

14. Increase effective communication with partner regarding childbearing/rearing decisions. (26, 27)

15. Recognize and accept that childbearing/rearing decisions are personal and that many different scenarios exist. (28)

21. Refer the client to a support group to reduce feeling of isolation (e.g., support group for infertility).

22. Conduct a family session that focuses on negotiating and reassigning roles and responsibilities among family members.

23. Help the client to develop a schedule and division of home responsibilities with partner.

24. Assist the client and partner in drawing a genogram while the couple explains the conflict in order to identify family-of-origin issues that may affect the childbearing/rearing conflict.

25. Ask each partner to define the meaning of the conflict regarding childbearing/rearing and the impact it has had on him or her personally and the relationship.

26. Help the partners practice overtly discussing possible solutions to their conflict and evaluate the associated pros and cons.

27. Help the partners practice expressing appreciation for the other partner's willingness to commit to working on potential solutions.

28. Assist the client with accepting her childbearing/rearing decision as "right" for her, while acknowledging that her attitudes may change with time.

—. _____
_____

—. _____
_____

—. _____   —. _____

 _____   _____

—. _____   —. _____

 _____   _____

DIAGNOSTIC SUGGESTIONS:

Axis I:	309.24	Adjustment Disorder with Anxiety
	309.0	Adjustment Disorder with Depressed Mood
	309.28	Adjustment Disorder with Mixed Anxiety and Depressed Mood
	300.4	Dysthymic Disorder
	V61.10	Partner Relational Problem
	V61.20	Parent-Child Relational Problem
	_____	_____
	_____	_____
Axis II:	301.81	Narcissistic Personality Disorder
	V71.09	No Diagnosis
	799.9	Diagnosis Deferred
	_____	_____
	_____	_____

DEPRESSION

Chapter co-authored with Danica G. Hays, PhD and Anneliese A. Singh, MS

BEHAVIORAL DEFINITIONS

1. Demonstrates dysphoric affect (e.g., sadness, hopelessness, helplessness, guilt, shame).
2. Evidences impaired ability to concentrate or make decisions.
3. Demonstrates an inability to accomplish daily tasks at a previous level at home, work, and/or academic settings.
4. Reports fatigue or lack of energy.
5. Evidences diminished interest or pleasure in current and future activities.
6. Demonstrates poor physical hygiene and grooming.
7. Describes somatic symptoms (e.g., changes in sleep, appetite, and/or sexual patterns; weight loss; headaches; pains; psychomotor agitation or retardation).
8. Reports irritability and/or crying spells.
9. Verbalizes difficulty coping adequately with stress and conflict related to multiple roles (e.g., partner, caretaker, worker, student).
10. Evidences suicidal ideation and/or gestures.
11. Describes poor interpersonal exchanges (e.g., isolation, loneliness, relationship distress).
12. Demonstrates mood-related delusions or hallucinations.

__. _____

_____

__. _____

_____

__. _____

_____

LONG-TERM GOALS

1. Improve depressed mood to maximize effective social, occupational, and physical functioning.
2. Develop healthy cognitive mechanisms to facilitate positive attitudes and beliefs about self within the context of one's environment to mitigate depressive symptoms.
3. Identify and increase intrapersonal, interpersonal, and physical resources to foster positive coping strategies.
4. Understand the relationships among women's roles, gender socialization, cultural background, and depression.

—. _____

_____

—. _____

_____

—. _____

_____

SHORT-TERM OBJECTIVES	THERAPEUTIC INTERVENTIONS
1. Articulate signs and symptoms of depression in current life experiences. (1)	1. Develop and nurture a safe and trusting therapeutic relationship; explore and validate the frequency, duration, and intensity of depressive symptoms.
2. Identify precipitating events and factors of depression, particularly roles of self and others in depression. (2, 3, 4, 5, 6)	2. Encourage the client to share her feelings of depression to gain an insight into precipitating events and implications of symptoms; normalize her feelings of depression.
	3. Encourage the client to describe current and childhood experiences associated with key relationships (e.g., family-of-origin, peer and school relationships, dating relationships, female role models, extended family

relationships), roles (e.g., partner, caretaker, worker, student), and cultural experiences (e.g., gender roles) that may contribute to depression.

4. Evaluate historical influences on current depressive symptoms, including previous episodes of depression, treatment history, and family history.

5. Explore the degree to which primary symptoms of depression are a result of gender role socialization (e.g., passivity, decreased self-esteem, learned helplessness, interpersonal orientation towards pleasing others).

6. Evaluate symptoms to consider the presence of culture-bound syndromes and/or culture specificity of symptoms (e.g., *ataques de nervios*, *amok*, *postemigration* effects).

3. Identify and replace cognitive self-talk that supports depression. (7, 8, 9, 10)

7. Encourage the client to discuss cognitive distortions, including automatic thoughts (e.g., negative view of self, future, experience) and negative schemas (e.g., core beliefs about self and others based on earlier childhood experiences); assess frequency of negative self-statements associated with depression.

8. Assign the client to keep a daily journal of automatic thoughts associated with depressive feelings (e.g., "Negative Thoughts Trigger Negative Feelings" in the *Adult Psychotherapy Homework Planner*, 2nd ed. by Jongsma;

"Daily Record of Dysfunctional Thoughts" in *Cognitive Therapy of Depression* by Beck, Rush, Shaw, and Emery); process the journal material to challenge depressive thinking patterns and replace them with reality-based thoughts.

9. Do "behavioral experiments" in which depressive automatic thoughts are treated as hypotheses/predictions, reality-based alternative hypotheses/predictions are generated, and both are tested against the client's past, present, and/or future experiences.

10. Reinforce the client's positive, reality-based cognitive messages that enhance self-confidence and increase adaptive action (see "Positive Self-Talk" in the *Adult Psychotherapy Homework Planner,* 2nd ed. by Jongsma).

4. Complete psychological testing to understand the severity of depressive symptoms. (11)

11. Administer to the client objective depression inventories (e.g., Beck Depression Inventory or Modified Scale for Suicidal Ideation); integrate results with other client information and provide feedback to the client.

5. Articulate any present suicide ideation, plan, and/or intent; verbalize any history of suicidal thoughts and/or gestures. (12, 13)

12. Assess the client's current level of risk for suicide. Explore any previous suicide attempts. Reduce risk for suicide by removing access and engaging in a safety contract.

13. Arrange for hospitalization, as necessary, when the client is judged to be harmful to self.

6. Take medications as prescribed by a physician and report any changes in mood or behavior. (14, 15)

7. Understand and articulate how symptoms of depression compare to current clinical and research trends of depression for women. (16)

8. Articulate counseling goals as well as additional treatment needs focused on reducing depression. (17, 18, 19)

14. Arrange for a physician to provide a medical and psychiatric evaluation to assess the client's need for antidepressant medications, rule out biomedical causes of depression, and prescribe medication if appropriate.

15. Monitor the client's compliance with medications, as well as potential side effects and effectiveness of medications; explore the client's level of satisfaction with integrating medication into her treatment plan.

16. Demystify the client's experiences with depression and reduce associated stigma; provide psychoeducation regarding signs and symptoms of depression (e.g., what is depression; who gets depressed; causes of depression; how behaviors, thoughts, and situational factors affect depression; treatment approaches).

17. Encourage the client to take an active role in the client's conceptualization and treatment of her depression.

18. Educate the client on available options to supplement counseling along with potential implications (e.g., couples and family therapy, support networks, financial support).

19. Collaborate with the client to develop concrete short- and long-term goals to decrease depression, considering personal and interpersonal advantages

9. Identify and replace previous and current life gender messages that have been antecedents of a depressive episode. (20, 21, 22, 23)

associated with goals and treatment needs; review goals periodically.

20. Assist the client in developing a list of negative messages about women that have reinforced her symptoms of depression; request that the client outline her behaviors and feelings associated with the negative messages.

21. Assess the client's beliefs about appropriate gender-role behaviors for women, as well as any feelings of role conflict that she may be experiencing.

22. Assign the client to keep a daily journal of intrapersonal and interpersonal experiences related to gender role messages, including affective and behavioral responses to these experiences; process the journal entries and conduct reality-testing to reframe any negative experiences and thoughts.

23. Engage the client in cognitive-restructuring exercises by which irrational beliefs about gender role are replaced with positive self-talk and reframing statements; assess perceived costs and benefits associated with distorted thinking.

10. Increase the frequency of engaging in pleasant activities. (24)

24. Engage the client in "behavioral activation" by scheduling activities that have a high likelihood for pleasure and mastery (see "Identify and Schedule Pleasant Activities" in the *Adult Psychotherapy Homework Planner,* 2nd ed. by Jongsma); use rehearsal,

roleplaying, or role reversal, as needed, to assist adoption in the client' daily life; reinforce success.

11. Report no longer having thoughts of self-harm. (25)

25. Periodically assess and monitor the client for suicide potential; intervene as necessary.

12. Develop healthy sleeping, eating, and grooming habits. (26)

26. Monitor and encourage the client to attend to personal grooming and healthy sleeping and eating patterns; reinforce improvement.

13. Read at least one self-help book addressing depression in women. (27)

27. Assign the client reading materials regarding overcoming depression for women (e.g., *Women and Depression: A Practical Self-Help Guide* by Sanders; *Feeling Good* by Burns; *Women & Depression* by Rosenthal; *Silencing the Self: Women and Depression* by Jack).

14. Seek out a positive female role model to empower self and increase self-care options. (28)

28. Empower the client to connect with a positive female role model through bibliotherapy and/or with family members, friends, or community leaders; review how the client may apply the adaptive behaviors of the role model to her own life.

15. Identify and articulate at least five positive statements about identity as a woman and the future. (29)

29. Assist the client to increase feelings of hopefulness by developing a list of positive characteristics about herself and her future; assign her to review this list daily.

16. Implement behavioral interventions to overcome depression. (30)

30. Teach the client stress management techniques (e.g., progressive muscle relaxation, deep breathing, guided imagery, spirituality).

17. Implement assertiveness to communicate needs and desires to others. (31, 32)

31. Provide assertiveness training, role-playing with the client different ways of coping with and

addressing situational stress; refer her to structured assertiveness training classes if necessary.

32. Assist the client to reevaluate priorities shaping her daily life, encouraging her to set limits on the scope of everyday activities (e.g., caretaking, employment, division of household labor, schoolwork) to minimize stress in a way that facilitates personal empowerment.

18. Implement conflict resolution skills to alleviate interpersonal sources of depressed mood. (33, 34, 35, 36)

33. Explore the role of interpersonal conflict in maintaining the client's depression; clarify the sources and nature of these conflicts.

34. Assign the client to write letters to individuals who may be contributing to her distress and depression, asking that she outline what she wants in the letters; process the letters, generating solutions within an interpersonal context.

35. Teach the client conflict resolution skills (e.g., empathy, active listening, "I messages," respectful communication, assertiveness without aggression, compromise) to help alleviate depression; use modeling, role-playing, and behavior rehearsal to work through several current conflicts.

36. Help the client resolve depression related to interpersonal problems through the use of reassurance and support, clarification of cognitive and affective triggers that ignite conflicts, and active problem-solving (or assign

"Applying Problem-Solving to Interpersonal Conflict" in the *Adult Psychotherapy Homework Planner,* 2nd ed. by Jongsma).

19. Increase social contacts and communicate needs within existing interpersonal relationships. (37, 38, 39)

37. Engage the client in social skills training as a means toward increasing a sense of personal power.

38. Encourage new interpersonal exchanges and assist the client in selecting satisfactory social experiences.

39. Reinforce the client's participation in social and interpersonal exchanges and monitor her adjustment to new situations; request that she verbalize thoughts and feelings associated with these experiences.

20. Increase the level of physical exercise. (40)

40. Assign the client to participate as fully as possible in a healthy exercise regimen.

21. Articulate self-care methods to prevent and/or manage depression in the future; create a list of 10 coping methods for future use. (41, 42, 43)

41. Assist the client to consider upcoming stressors; brainstorm with her 10 ways to mitigate depression in the future.

42. Encourage the client to continue participation in positive social support systems.

43. Offer the client booster sessions as necessary.

—. _____

_____

—. _____

_____

—. _____

_____

—. _____

_____

—. _____

_____

—. _____

_____

DIAGNOSTIC SUGGESTIONS:

Axis I:	296.xx	Major Depressive Disorder
	300.4	Dysthymic Disorder
	311	Depressive Disorder NOS
	296.xx	Bipolar I Disorder
	296.89	Bipolar II Disorder
	301.13	Cyclothymic Disorder
	296.90	Mood Disorder NOS
	309.0	Adjustment Disorder with Depressed Mood
	295.70	Schizoaffective Disorder
	V62.81	Relational Problem NOS
	V62.82	Bereavement
	V62.89	Phase of Life Problem
	_____	_____
	_____	_____
Axis II:	301.9	Personality Disorder NOS (Depressive)
	V71.09	No Diagnosis
	799.9	Diagnosis Deferred
	_____	_____
	_____	_____

DIVORCE

BEHAVIORAL DEFINITIONS

1. Reports anger, resentment, irritability, loneliness, and grief related to a divorce.
2. Evidences depression and anxiety-related symptoms (e.g., impaired decision-making ability, sleep disturbances, problems with concentration).
3. Experiences trauma symptoms associated with a marriage characterized by abuse and/or manipulation.
4. Avoids interpersonal relationships during and after divorce proceedings.
5. Verbalizes difficulty in coping with everyday stressors during and after a divorce.
6. Expresses anxiety and stress associated with financial situation after or during a divorce.
7. Experiences stress and anxiety related to a potential loss-of-custody battle due to previous mental health issues or concerns (e.g., documented hospitalizations for mental health issues, prescribed psychotropic medication) or manipulations of ex-spouse.
8. Experiences stress associated with difficulties negotiating with ex-spouse on issues related to children (e.g., visitation, child support, discipline, stepfamilies).
9. Verbalizes concern for social exclusion from affiliations, organizations, and interpersonal relationships due to impending divorce.
10. Experiences stress and feelings of hopelessness due to negotiating the legal system.
11. Divorce is pending and feelings of fear, anger, and rejection are reported.

—. _____
_____
—. _____
_____
—. _____
_____

LONG-TERM GOALS

1. Accept the reality of divorce.
2. Resolve negative feelings associated with the divorce (e.g., guilt, anger, anxiety, loss).
3. Negotiate personal relationships and redefine boundaries.
4. Commit to the process of self-affirmation and personal growth.
5. Establish an effective parental role.
6. Develop a stable positive identity independent of the former spousal relationship.

—. _____
_____
—. _____
_____
—. _____
_____

SHORT-TERM OBJECTIVES

1. Discuss the events surrounding the divorce and related feelings and behavior. (1)

2. Explore and process intense feelings of guilt, grief, anger, shame, and anxiety surrounding the divorce and its impact. (2, 3)

THERAPEUTIC INTERVENTIONS

1. Develop and nurture a safe and trusting therapeutic relationship; explore the client's perception of the deterioration of the marriage relationship and ultimate divorce.

2. Explore and validate the client's feelings associated with the divorce.

3. Assign the client to read *How to Survive the Loss of a Love* by Colgrove, Bloomfield, and McWilliams; discuss the client's reactions to the book and process.

3. Explore and process feelings of isolation and rejection, including those of betrayal associated with a breach of trust or infidelity/extramarital relations. (4)

4. Explore the client's potential feelings of betrayal and dejection associated with a breach of trust or abandonment.

4. Explore and understand sociocultural influences on attitudes toward marriage and divorce. (5, 6)

5. Explore the degree to which the client's cultural background impacts her values and attitudes regarding marriage; explore the positive and negative implications of these messages for her life.

6. Assist the client in learning to evaluate and subsequently understand expectations and disappointments associated with her marriage.

5. Identify and challenge dysfunctional thoughts associated with the divorce. (7, 8)

7. Encourage the client to explore, challenge, and replace cognitive distortions and negative schemas related to divorce that contribute to self-blame and stagnation (e.g., "I am a failure because my marriage failed"; "I will never have a satisfying relationship"; "I will never get over this").

8. Explore with the client dysfunctional thoughts and provide her with tools to challenge such thoughts; help her change her belief from demands (e.g., "We must not divorce") to desires (e.g., "I prefer not to divorce") and from perceiving the divorce and/or its accompanying circumstances as devastating to

disappointing (or assign "Negative Thoughts Trigger Negative Feelings" in the *Adult Psychotherapy Homework Planner,* 2nd ed. by Jongsma).

6. Implement stress management techniques to reduce debilitating emotional and somatic symptoms. (9, 10)

9. Educate the client on the relationship between divorce-related stressors self-esteem, depression, anxiety, and somatic symptoms.

10. Educate the client on stress management techniques (e.g., eating nutritiously, decreasing caffeine and alcohol, sleeping, exercising, using deep muscle relaxation, journaling).

7. Identify at least one person willing to listen and provide support. (11)

11. Encourage and help the client to build a support network; brainstorm sources of support (e.g., clergy, close family, recently divorced friends) and methods to use (e.g., call and invite a friend for lunch).

8. Become more adept at working with the legal system and attorneys. (12, 13, 14)

12. Assign the client relevant reading materials and web sites related to the legalities of divorce (e.g., *What Every Woman Should Know About Divorce and Custody* by Smith and Abrahms; *Constructive Divorce: Procedural Justice and Sociolegal Reform* by Bryan; www.womansdivorce .com).

13. Refer the client to a divorce group and seminars related to negotiating the practical aspects of divorce and the legal system.

14. Validate the client's frustrations associated with negotiating the legal system and help her to develop relevant coping strategies (e.g., establishing a support

system, using relaxation exercises, setting aside time each day when the divorce process is not the focus).

9. Identify ways of managing financial obligations. (15)

15. Help the client explore ways to manage her money, pursue child support payments, and potentially seek educational and/or career training.

10. Develop a plan to address multiple life demands associated with the divorce that require attention. (16)

16. Assist the client with daily activities (e.g., changing car titles of ownership, relocating, negotiating relationships with children).

11. Explore and identify at least three ways to handle increased parental obligations associated with single parenthood. (17, 18)

17. Brainstorm, along with the client, ways to manage increased parental obligations and make her life more manageable and less stressful (see Single Parenting chapter in this *Planner*).

18. Refer the client to a single mother support group.

12. Establish effective parenting skills; stabilize new lifestyle and daily routine for children. (19, 20)

19. Role-play with the client effective parenting techniques; refer the client to books (e.g., *Parenting Through Change* by Forgatch) and videos on effective parenting (see Single Parenting chapter in this *Planner*).

20. Use a Parent Management Training approach beginning with teaching the client how parent and child behavioral interactions can encourage or discourage positive or negative behavior and how changing key elements of those interactions (e.g., prompting and reinforcing positive behaviors) can be used to promote positive change (e.g., *Parenting the Strong-Willed Child* by Forehand and Long).

13. Implement effective approaches to negotiating childcare and co-parenting with ex-spouse. (21, 22)

21. Explore, along with the client, ways to negotiate with the noncustodial parent in ways that minimize conflict and stress; help the client to develop bargaining and conflict resolution skills.

22. Role-play with the client ways of negotiating childcare and co-parenting with ex-spouse.

14. Engage in at least one consciousness-raising activity and verbalize a sense of personal mastery. (23, 24, 25)

23. Help the client to develop confidence and mastery by identifying her strengths and accomplishments.

24. Refer the client to a consciousness-raising support group.

25. Educate the client on available options to supplement individual counseling (e.g., group counseling, family therapy, bibliotherapy, art therapy).

15. Participate in enjoyable activities that can be engaged in alone at least once per week. (26)

26. Brainstorm enjoyable and relaxing activities that the client may engage in regularly (or assign "Identify and Schedule Pleasant Activities" in the *Adult Psychotherapy Homework Planner,* 2nd ed. by Jongsma).

16. Establish and redefine boundaries with family members, friends, and acquaintances. (27)

27. Role-play with the client ways of establishing relationship boundaries with her ex-spouse, family members, friends, and acquaintances; help the client develop skills to negotiate her extended family's reactions to the divorce.

17. Transition from focusing on the negative aspects of the divorce to the benefits/positive consequences associated with the divorce. (28)

28. Help the client to explore the positive consequences associated with a divorce (e.g., end of an abusive relationship, opportunity for growth).

18. Verbalize an identity and plans as a single person rather than a divorcee/ex-spouse. (29, 30, 31)

19. Focus positively on the future and learn to develop satisfying roles and lifestyle. (32, 33)

29. Assist the client in clarifying her values and goals as part of the process of rebuilding a "single person" identity.

30. Help the client develop realistic expectations and skills for relationship formation as a new single person.

31. Encourage the client to attend programs/groups that address anxieties dealing with forming new relationships.

32. Reassure the client that the journey may be "long and arduous," and a slow recuperation phase is normal.

33. Assist the client in creating new dreams and goals and a realistic plan of how to achieve them; emphasize the thought "There is life after divorce!"

___. _____   ___. _____
    _____   _____
___. _____   ___. _____
    _____   _____
___. _____   ___. _____
    _____   _____

DIAGNOSTIC SUGGESTIONS:

Axis I:
309.0	Adjustment Disorder with Depressed Mood
309.24	Adjustment Disorder with Anxiety
309.28	Adjustment Disorder with Mixed Anxiety and Depressed Mood
V61.1	Partner Relational Problem
309.21	Separation Anxiety Disorder
V62.89	Phase of Life Problem

_____ _____

_____ _____

Axis II:	301.6	Dependent Personality Disorder
	V71.09	No Diagnosis
	799.9	Diagnosis Deferred
	_____	_____
	_____	_____

DOMESTIC VIOLENCE/BATTERY

BEHAVIORAL DEFINITIONS

1. Has experienced physical assault committed by a current or former intimate partner.
2. Has experienced emotional abuse and control (e.g., humiliation, insults, isolation from friends and family, financial control).
3. Reports fear of imminent physical harm because of prior bodily injury, assault, or threats.
4. Feels controlled and coerced by a partner (to stay in the relationship) through physical, sexual, and/or emotional violence and threats (e.g., use of violence, suicide, threaten to take away the children).

—. _____
   _____
—. _____
   _____
—. _____
   _____

LONG-TERM GOALS

1. Develop sense of own personal power, self-esteem, and control; reduce feelings of helplessness.
2. Eliminate self-blame and increase understanding that the partner is solely responsible for violent and abusive behavior.
3. Recognize the cycle and pattern of violence and identify warning signs for future relationships.
4. Understand the costs and benefits of remaining in or terminating an abusive relationship.

5. Reduce or eliminate Posttraumatic Stress Disorder (PTSD) symptoms and depression.
6. Establish long-term safety for self and children.

—. _____

_____

—. _____

_____

—. _____

_____

SHORT-TERM OBJECTIVES

THERAPEUTIC INTERVENTIONS

1. Verbalize the frequency and severity of the current and past abuse, batterer's access to weapons, and batterer's use of drugs/alcohol. (1, 2, 3)

1. Create a safe therapeutic environment where the client can disclose the nature of the abuse experience.

2. Document the client's complaints of abuse verbatim, take a complete medical, family, and relationship history, and note sources of social support.

3. Document the client's past and current injuries, the nature of threats, current level of fear, and criminal justice interventions previously tried.

2. Verbalize behavioral definitions of physical and psychological abuse. (4, 5)

4. Assist the client in defining physical and emotional abuse in concrete, behavioral terms.

5. Educate the client that partner abuse is illegal and maladaptive to her psychological and physical health.

3. Establish a safety plan that identifies a safe place to go for protection if violence erupts or becomes imminent. (6)

6. Help the client establish a safety plan that includes identifying all possible escape routes and a place to go, packing a survival kit,

4. Verbalize an awareness of appropriate services and options located both within and external to the community. (7)

5. Identify at least two behaviors that typically signal an escalation toward violence. (8)

6. Verbalize at least three negative effects of partner violence on self and children. (9, 10)

7. Explore the effects of cultural values, gender roles, economic and social mobility, and social isolation that may adversely impact proactive responses to abuse. (11)

starting an individual savings account, and keeping a telephone number of a domestic violence hotline; review and refine throughout therapy.

7. Refer the client to advocacy services (e.g., shelters, legal services, child protective services, transportation providers); encourage her to also seek the assistance of other non-mental health providers who are trained in domestic violence and represent the client's cultural milieu (e.g., religious or spiritual leaders, community leaders, health providers, extended family members).

8. Teach the client to recognize the gradations of anger and the behaviors and cognitions associated with it (e.g., irritation, disapproval, control, rage, denial).

9. Explore with the client the psychological, emotional, physical, and spiritual impact the abuse has on her and the children.

10. Educate the client regarding the immediate and future destructive consequences that partner abuse has (or can have) on her and on the children.

11. Explore the client's cultural values (e.g., family loyalty, shame) and social network, including acculturation level, that may negatively impact her willingness and ability to take action to end the abuse; explore the client's potential suspiciousness of the mental health system.

8. Identify three ways in which the abuser maintained power over the client and fostered feelings of helplessness. (12, 13)

9. Identify the relationship between the abuse experience and low self-esteem and feelings of powerlessness. (14)

10. Identify childhood experiences (including gender role messages) that taught the client that abuse is to be expected, excused, and tolerated. (15)

11. Eliminate self-blame; hold the abusive partner responsible for the abuse. (16, 17, 18)

12. Implement assertiveness and communication skills. (19, 20, 21)

12. Explore areas in the client's life in which the abuser maintained control and the resultant feelings of client helplessness.

13. Assist the client in identifying more adaptive, assertive responses to the partner's controlling behaviors.

14. Assist the client in identifying her negative beliefs about herself and how these were fostered by the abuser.

15. Explore the client's childhood experiences and socio-cultural messages (e.g., women should be passive; male violence should be tolerated) that fostered acceptance of abusive behavior.

16. Explore the client's pattern of blaming herself for her partner's abusive behavior, and teach her to take personal responsibility for only her behavioral decisions.

17. Confront the client's pattern of taking responsibility for the abusive partner's behavior; ask the client to report instances when violence occurred and she did not verbalize being at fault.

18. Reinforce the client for holding the abusive partner responsible for behavior.

19. Engage in assertiveness training with the client that includes her knowing her basic rights (e.g., self-respect); reinforce assertive behavior.

20. Assign the client the exercise of identifying her positive physical characteristics in a mirror to help

her become more comfortable with herself.

21. Ask the client to complete and process an exercise in the book *Ten Days to Self-Esteem!* (Burns).

13. Verbalize increased feelings of self-esteem and control over own life. (22, 23, 24, 25)

22. Assist the client in identifying personal and environmental obstacles to self-esteem (e.g., lack of assertiveness skills, unhealthy relationships, unresolved trauma).

23. Assist the client in becoming aware of how she indirectly expresses negative feelings about herself (e.g., lack of eye contact, social withdrawal, sweating, expectations of failure or rejection).

24. Discuss, emphasize, and interpret the client's incidents of abuse (i.e., emotional, physical, and sexual) and how they have impacted her feelings about herself.

25. Refer the client to an empowerment or therapy group that is focused on identifying strengths and increasing self-esteem/assertiveness.

14. Learn and implement three relaxation techniques. (26, 27, 28)

26. Educate the client on the relaxing, calming, and balancing benefits of practices such as yoga, meditation, and prayer; provide suggestions on how to get started (e.g., book, video, local gym class).

27. Train the client in the use of prescribed breathing or deep-muscle relaxation.

28. Practice relaxation techniques with the client in order to achieve mastery and apply them in real-life situations; role-play real-life situations in which relaxation can be used profitably.

15. Identify situations and cues that could trigger a return to the abusive partner. (29)

29. Help the client identify situations that may pull her back into the battery situation (e.g., financial troubles, fantasies, feelings of love for her batterer); encourage her to utilize alternative coping strategies (e.g., develop social support, identify and challenge self-defeating thoughts, engage in activities that foster empowerment).

16. Increase coping and decision-making effectiveness. (30, 31, 32)

30. Educate the client on the residual effects of domestic violence (e.g., decreased decision-making and problem-solving skills).

31. Identify past coping behavior (e.g., attempts at self-care that have gone awry), what has been tried previously as solutions, what has been helpful, and what has been unsuccessful; facilitate effective coping and decision making.

32. Teach problem-solving strategies involving specifically defining a problem, generating options for addressing it, evaluating options, implementing a plan, and reevaluating and refining the plan.

17. Assess alternatives to the relationship and accept referrals regarding respite from or termination of the relationship. (7, 33)

7. Refer the client to advocacy services (e.g., shelters, legal services, child protective services, transportation providers); encourage her to also seek the assistance of other non-

mental health providers who are trained in domestic violence and represent the client's cultural milieu (e.g., religious or spiritual leaders, community leaders, health providers, extended family members).

33. Assist the client in evaluating available alternatives to the current relationship.

__. _____   __. _____

_____   _____

__. _____   __. _____

_____   _____

__. _____   __. _____

_____   _____

DIAGNOSTIC SUGGESTIONS:

Axis I:	995.81	Physical Abuse of Adult, Victim
	300.4	Dysthymic Disorder
	296.xx	Major Depressive Disorder
	300.02	Generalized Anxiety Disorder
	309.81	Posttraumatic Stress Disorder
	300.14	Dissociative Identity Disorder
	303.90	Alcohol Dependence
	304.80	Polysubstance Dependence
	_____	_____
	_____	_____
Axis II:	301.82	Avoidant Personality Disorder
	301.83	Borderline Personality Disorder
	301.6	Dependent Personality Disorder
	V71.09	No Diagnosis
	799.9	Diagnosis Deferred
	_____	_____
	_____	_____

INFERTILITY

Chapter co-authored with Jane E. Frances-Fischer, PhD

BEHAVIORAL DEFINITIONS

1. Experiences persistent loss, grief, and dysphoric/depressive affect (e.g., hopelessness, helplessness, worthlessness, pessimism, guilt, shame) due to inability to have children.
2. Lacks interest in usual activities and has strained interpersonal relationships.
3. Reports difficulty concentrating and constant preoccupation with thoughts of infertility, leading to disruption in daily functioning and diminished ability to accomplish tasks.
4. Presents with changes in sleeping patterns, appetite, and/or weight.
5. Engages in increased use of recreational drugs or alcohol.
6. Evidences suicidal ideation and/or gestures.
7. Experiences social isolation, loneliness, and/or alienation when exposed to environments/social situations that include families and children.
8. Reports persistent feelings of bitterness and/or anger over inability to produce a child.
9. Reports anxiety, irritability, agitation, increased emotionality, and/or crying spells due to lack of reproductive control.
10. Lacks sexual desire and satisfaction as sexual focus is on procreation, not pleasure.
11. Experiences diminished self-esteem due to inability to achieve pregnancy leading to childbirth.

—. _____
   _____

—. _____
   _____

—. _____
   _____

LONG-TERM GOALS

1. Develop and implement effective behavioral cognitive and affective coping strategies to deal with reproductive failures, resultant emotional issues, and interpersonal stressors.
2. Understand the relationship among women's roles, gender socialization, cultural background, and expectations for fertility, pregnancy, and childbearing.
3. Increase knowledge and awareness of infertility medical diagnoses, procedures and medications indicated in the treatment of infertility, and their potential physical and psychological effects.
4. Become educated about and explore family-building options including a variety of medical treatments, adoption, third-party reproduction, and child-free living.

—. _____
_____
—. _____
_____
—. _____
_____

SHORT-TERM OBJECTIVES	THERAPEUTIC INTERVENTIONS
1. Describe in detail the infertility story, including lifetime hopes, plans, and dreams of pregnancy, childbirth, and parenting. (1, 2, 3, 4)	1. Develop a safe and trusting therapeutic relationship through active listening and unconditional positive regard.
	2. Provide empathy, compassion, and nonjudgmental support as the client is encouraged to tell in detail her infertility story.
	3. Encourage the client to express both thoughts and feelings; validate emotions, and assist the client in identifying and verbalizing feelings generated by infertility.

2. Acknowledge the personal meaning, significance, and reality of infertility and articulate counseling goals. (5, 6)

3. Identify ways to attain emotional balance. (7, 8, 9)

4. Cooperate with a referral for a psychotropic medication evaluation. (10)

5. Acknowledge the reality of infertility as a medical condition and the probable need for medical treatment. (11, 12)

6. Implement problem-solving strategies regarding options of medical treatment for infertility. (13, 14, 15)

4. Provide reassurance about the normalcy of the client's feelings and reactions to infertility.

5. Inquire about the significance and personal meaning the client has constructed about her infertility issues.

6. Assist the client in articulating concrete goals for counseling regarding her feelings associated with her infertility.

7. Educate the client about the impact of infertility on psychological distress.

8. Assess the client for depression, anxiety mood disorders, and suicidal thoughts or behavior; inquire about recent changes in eating, sleeping, or work behaviors.

9. Use role-play to teach the client skills for emotional regulation (e.g., identify and challenge automatic negative thoughts).

10. Recommend, if necessary, a psychiatric consultation for a medication evaluation for emotional stabilization.

11. Validate the client's realization of the impact of infertility.

12. Present a realistic view of infertility medical treatment and educate the client about treatment options and their current success rates.

13. Assist the client in assessing the pros and cons of specific medical treatment options for infertility (e.g., explore third-party reproduction, adoption, and child-free living).

7. Verbalize concrete goals for infertility medical treatment and desired outcome. (16, 17)

8. Read self-help books about infertility to better understand the emotional experience and medical treatment options, reduce isolation, and increase sense of hope. (18, 19)

9. Develop and sustain supportive relationships with friends or family members. (20)

14. Prepare the client through support and education for the realities of infertility treatment.

15. Encourage the client to explore reproductive technologies that result in nongestational and/or nongenetic parenthood.

16. Assist the client in increasing feelings of hopefulness by generating a list of specific goals, plans, priorities, and strategies for infertility medical treatment.

17. Encourage the client to engage in couples counseling with her spouse or partner to jointly determine infertility treatment goal setting.

18. Ask the client to read at least three books about infertility (e.g., *The Infertility Survival Guide: Everything You Need to Know to Cope With the Challenges While Maintaining Your Sanity, Dignity and Relationships* by Daniluk; *Experiencing Infertility: An Essential Resource* by Peoples and Rovner-Ferguson; *Conquering Infertility: Dr. Alice Domar's Mind/Body Guide to Enhancing Fertility and Coping With Infertility* by Domar and Kelly); process the content with the client.

19. Encourage the client to ask her spouse, partner, or family members to read at least two books on infertility and to share their feelings and reactions with the client.

20. Encourage the client to reach out to supportive individuals who provide empathy and concern regarding infertility issues.

10. Engage in social and recreational activities that are positive and uplifting. (21, 22)

21. Reinforce the client's participation in social and interpersonal exchanges; encourage the client to seek out spiritual activities and communities to increase her sense of support, relieve social isolation, and encourage hopefulness.

22. Engage the client in "behavioral activation" by scheduling activities that have a high likelihood for pleasure and mastery (see "Identify and Schedule Pleasant Activities" in the *Adult Psychotherapy Homework Planner,* 2nd ed. by Jongsma); use rehearsal, role-playing, role reversal, as needed, to assist adoption in the client's daily life; reinforce success.

11. Attend local and/or national infertility support organizations. (23)

23. Recommend the client attend monthly meetings and/or infertility support groups that provide education, information, and advocacy to relieve a sense of isolation; process experiences, support, and practical insights gained.

12. Implement behavioral stress-reduction skills and self-care methods. (24, 25)

24. Help the client learn to manage the stresses of infertility by teaching relaxation techniques, coping methods for dealing with strong emotions (e.g., cognitive restructuring, meditation), and mechanisms to relieve the physical symptoms of stress (e.g., yoga, focused breathing, healthy diet).

25. Teach the client to implement specific stress management coping mechanisms (e.g., maintaining a daily journal of

cognitive, affective, and behavioral experiences related to infertility; practicing deep-breathing exercises once a day; doing yoga, meditation, or other daily physical exercise for at least 30 minutes; establishing daily healthy sleeping patterns; eating a balanced and nutritious diet); review implementation, reinforcing success and redirecting for failure.

13. Identify and replace distorted cognitive messages associated with infertility. (26, 27, 28)

26. Assist the client in identifying her unrealistic, distorted messages of low self-worth, guilt, shame, and responsibility related to infertility.

27. Assist the client in reframing and restructuring her thoughts with more realistic, constructive messages.

28. Reinforce the client's positive, reality-based cognitive messages that enhance self-confidence and increase adaptive action (see "Positive Self-Talk" in the *Adult Psychotherapy Homework Planner,* 2nd ed. by Jongsma).

14. Identify and explore gendered reactions to infertility and medical treatment and its relationship to internalized socio-cultural messages. (29, 30)

29. Encourage the client to describe childhood and current reproductive messages received from family and society (e.g., when to get partnered or married, when to have children, how many children to have, how to parent).

30. Help the client to understand potentially different emotional reactions of males and females to infertility, as well as the use of varied coping techniques due to gender-role socialization and internalized cultural values.

15. Describe primary relationship stressors that dealing with infertility has created. (31)

16. Verbalize sexual attitudes, feelings, and experiences that have become dysfunctional as a result of infertility. (32, 33)

17. Express the decision to end unsuccessful infertility treatment and redefine the meaning of family. (34, 35)

18. Achieve a successful adjustment to pregnancy after infertility. (36, 37)

31. Inquire about the client's marital/primary relationship status and problems arising as a result of dealing with infertility; process cognitive and affective responses, and work on active problem-solving strategies.

32. Support the client in exploring the impact of infertility on the sexual relationship with her spouse/ significant other.

33. Enlist the client to openly communicate her feelings and needs to her partner; encourage the development of coping strategies (e.g., relaxation skills, assertiveness skills, stress management, reframing, humor) to reduce interpersonal conflict, decrease stress, and return their sexual relationship to a healthy level of functioning.

34. Explore and process the client's feelings and facilitate decision making regarding terminating infertility treatment; help the client prepare for an outcome without children.

35. Process the options of adoption, fostering children, and child-free living.

36. Acknowledge and process the client's potential emotional reaction from pregnancy after infertility (e.g., denial, fear, overprotection of self).

37. Provide continued support and help the client strengthen coping mechanisms when faced with excessive worry, doubt, and/or potential physical risks/

19. Achieve a successful adjustment to parenting after infertility. (38, 39, 40, 41)

complications due to pregnancy after infertility treatment.

38. Acknowledge and support the client's ongoing processing of unique issues faced by parents after infertility (e.g., older age, same-sex parenting, single parenting, having twins or multiples, adopting children, and/or children created through medical treatment, third-party reproduction, or surrogacy); reinforce adaptive and healthy planning.

39. Provide the client with basic parenting skills information and training, including the developmental stages of both parents and children.

40. Recommend that the client read parenting books (e.g., *Adopting After Infertility* by Johnston; *The Long- Awaited Stork: A Guide to Parenting After Infertility* by Glazer; *Mommy Did I Grow in Your Tummy? Where Babies Come From* by Gordon) and utilize online resources dealing with parenting issues (e.g., the American Fertility Association's web site [www.theafa.org], the American Society of Reproductive Medicine's web site [www.asrm.org], the National Infertility Association's web site [www.resolve.org]).

41. Encourage the client to think about and process how she will deal with her child's unique origins in terms of methods of disclosure to the child, friends, family, and community.

___. _____   ___. _____

_____   _____

___. _____   ___. _____

_____   _____

___. _____   ___. _____

_____   _____

DIAGNOSTIC SUGGESTIONS:

Axis I: 296.xx Major Depressive Disorder
300.02 Generalized Anxiety Disorder
300.4 Dysthymic Disorder
309.28 Adjustment Disorder with Mixed Anxiety and Depressed Mood
309.0 Adjustment Disorder with Depressed Mood
V61.9 Relational Problem Related to Infertility

_____ _____

_____ _____

Axis II: V71.09 No Diagnosis
799.9 Diagnosis Deferred

_____ _____

_____ _____

LOW SELF-ESTEEM/LACK OF ASSERTIVENESS

Chapter co-authored with Karia Kelch-Oliver, MS

BEHAVIORAL DEFINITIONS

1. Verbalizes self-disparaging remarks and devalued opinion of self and abilities.
2. Constantly seeks appraisals and approval from others to validate self-worth.
3. Demonstrates difficulty accepting compliments and identifying positive attributes.
4. Demonstrates difficulty identifying and expressing needs and desires.
5. Demonstrates difficulty saying "no" to others due to fear of rejection.
6. Demonstrates difficulty defending her rights.
7. Demonstrates difficulty establishing autonomy and resisting group or individual pressure toward conformity.
8. Lacks initiative to take action to resolve problems and to satisfy needs.
9. Evidences difficulty leading, directing, and influencing others.

—. _____

_____

—. _____

_____

—. _____

_____

LONG-TERM GOALS

1. Reduce self-disparaging remarks and negative self-talk.
2. Improve self-esteem and develop a positive self-image as capable and competent.
3. Increase ability to express needs and desires openly and honestly.

4. Increase assertiveness skills and ability to advocate for self.
5. Increase involvement in activities that foster confidence and a sense of accomplishment.
6. Increase openness to experiences and opportunities associated with risk-taking.

—. _____

_____

—. _____

_____

—. _____

_____

SHORT-TERM OBJECTIVES

1. Describe personal history of self-devaluation and lack of assertiveness. (1)

2. Acknowledge self-disparaging statements and recognize the tendency to engage in such statements. (2, 3)

3. Decrease the frequency of making self-disparaging remarks. (4, 5, 6)

THERAPEUTIC INTERVENTIONS

1. Discuss context of self-disparagement, including client's perceptions of self from childhood to present, role of caregivers and peers, and related experiences.

2. Assist the client in identifying negative beliefs about herself.

3. Assist the client in becoming aware of how she indirectly expresses negative feelings about self (e.g., lack of eye contact, social withdrawal, sweating, expectations of failure or rejection).

4. Use cognitive-restructuring techniques to change the client's belief system (i.e., via reality-testing and rational thought) toward a more positive, realistic self-perception.

5. Refer the client to an empowerment or therapy group that is focused on identifying strengths and increasing self-esteem/assertiveness.

6. Ask the client to complete and process an exercise in the book *Ten Days to Self-Esteem!* (Burns).

4. Identify at least three positive personal attributes. (7, 8, 9)

7. Ask the client to make a list including positive qualities about herself and accomplishments; verbally reinforce positive self-statements.

8. Encourage the client to make at least one positive statement about herself during the therapy session.

9. Assist the client in developing a list of positive affirmations to be read three times a day or to be put on a mirror at home.

5. Verbalize an understanding of the differences between passive, assertive, and aggressive behavior. (10)

10. Assign the client to read *Your Perfect Right: Assertiveness and Equality in Your Life and Relationships* by Alberti and Emmons; process the content to clarify the distinction between passivity, assertiveness, and aggression.

6. Identify three anxiety-related fears associated with being assertive. (11)

11. Explore the client's fears of being assertive (e.g., fear of rejection, fear of ineffectiveness, fear of ridicule).

7. Engage in two activities in which competence has been demonstrated in order to improve self-esteem. (12, 13)

12. Explore areas of competency with the client and encourage her to engage in related activities (e.g., dance, singing, arts, volunteer work, joining a book club).

13. Encourage participation in physical activities that foster

8. Identify three roadblocks to improved self-esteem. (14, 15)

9. Develop an awareness of female gender role socialization and its relationship to low self-esteem and lack of assertiveness. (16, 17)

10. Identify one person who can serve as a model of assertiveness and a source of vicarious learning. (18, 19)

11. Practice saying "no" to at least one person, declining to

confidence and well-being (e.g., yoga, meditation, martial arts).

14. Assist the client in identifying intrapersonal and interpersonal obstacles to self-esteem (e.g., self-deprecating comments, perfectionism, unhealthy relationships).

15. Encourage the client to keep a journal in which she writes down her positive experiences and tracks her progress in building her self-esteem.

16. Explore with the client the messages she received growing up regarding appropriate behavior for girls and women and the degree to which she internalized these messages.

17. Assist the client with identifying gender role messages that are empowering and those that are limiting to her self-worth and assertiveness; facilitate her identifying and developing her own values.

18. Review with the client women in her social network who she perceives as assertive (therapist can serve as an assertiveness model for the client); help the client to identify behaviors demonstrated by the model that represent assertiveness.

19. Encourage the client to practice both in and out of the session the assertive behaviors that she was exposed to via the model.

20. Utilize role-play and in-session rehearsal to teach and assess the

comply with a request/favor or identify and assert rights, needs, and wants. (20, 21)

12. Implement at least one decision based on own beliefs and values. (22)

13. Verbalize three physiological signs of arousal that negatively affect one's self-esteem, successful completion of tasks, and ability to demonstrate assertiveness. (23, 24)

14. Recall situations in which beliefs and feelings were asserted. (25, 26)

15. Identify and strengthen connections to others who

client's assertiveness skills; reinforce progress.

21. Teach the client how to exercise her rights appropriately via assertiveness training.

22. Teach the client how to solve her problems more effectively and efficiently by identifying possible responses to situations and their likely outcomes, knowing how to select the best alternative given a particular situation, and having the ability to develop a realistic plan to reach that goal.

23. Educate the client to recognize internal anxiety cues in various settings and social situations (e.g., heart racing, sweating, muscle tension).

24. Teach the client three coping skills (e.g., deep-breathing exercises, muscle-relaxation techniques, stress management, meditation, and guided imagery) to combat the physiological cues of anxiety.

25. Encourage the client to pay particular attention to her inclinations and not immediately dismiss them; review situations in the recent past in which she discounted her thoughts and feelings.

26. Validate the client's feelings and encourage her attempts to listen to herself; reinforce experiences of asserting her rights and feelings.

27. Encourage the client to seek out situations and people that affirm

affirm self-esteem and respect one's assertiveness. (27)

her self-worth and avoid or limit her exposure to situations and people that are demeaning.

—. _____   —. _____

_____   _____

—. _____   —. _____

_____   _____

—. _____   —. _____

_____   _____

DIAGNOSTIC SUGGESTIONS:

Axis I: 300.4   Dysthymic Disorder
300.23   Social Phobia
296.xx   Major Depressive Disorder

_____ _____

_____ _____

Axis II: 301.6   Dependent Personality Disorder
301.82   Avoidant Personality Disorder
V71.09   No Diagnosis
799.9   Diagnosis Deferred

_____ _____

_____ _____

MENOPAUSE AND PERIMENOPAUSE

Chapter co-authored with Wendy Heath-Gainer, EdS

BEHAVIORAL DEFINITIONS

1. Experiences physiological indicators of menopause (e.g., hot flashes, heavy and/or irregular periods, vaginal dryness, night sweats, heart palpitations, migraine headaches, weight gain, fibroids, change in libido, urinary symptoms, breast swelling/tenderness, insomnia, skin changes).
2. Experiences anxiety or discomfort over the physical symptoms experienced during menopause as well as possible medical conditions such as osteoporosis.
3. Internalizes and verbalizes negative attitudes and a lowered self-esteem related to menopause and aging.
4. Verbalizes a diminished sense of personal attractiveness coupled with a shift in body shape and/or weight gain.
5. Reports feelings of anxiety over major decisions impacting physical and psychological well-being (e.g., whether or not to undergo hormone replacement therapy [HRT] or a hysterectomy).
6. Experiences depressive symptoms or mood shifts sometimes related to distressing symptoms or long perimenopause.
7. Evidences a loss of interest in sex or romantic relationships.
8. Diagnosed with premature ovarian failure (menopause symptoms occurring when less than 40 years old).

—. _____
_____

—. _____
_____

—. _____
_____

LONG-TERM GOALS

1. Adapt to the normal physical changes that occur with the onset and course of menopause.
2. Resolve the psychological effects of menopause, including depression, anxiety, and body image concerns.
3. Learn to differentiate between internal attitudes regarding the meaning of menopause from societal messages.
4. Develop comfort with own sexuality.

—. _____

_____

—. _____

_____

—. _____

_____

SHORT-TERM OBJECTIVES	THERAPEUTIC INTERVENTIONS
1. Verbalize the symptoms of menopause experienced, as well as when and how frequently they occur. (1, 2)	1. Cultivate a safe, trusting therapeutic environment through verbal and nonverbal displays of unconditional positive regard, warmth, empathy, and acceptance that facilitates the client's sharing as her menopause symptoms are explored.
	2. Ask the client to verbalize her assigned meaning of being perimenopausal or menopausal; communicate that each woman is unique in terms of when and how menopausal symptoms are experienced.

2. Develop a basic understanding of the course, challenges, and typical symptoms experienced during menopause. (3, 4, 5)

3. Assess the client's understanding of physical, emotional, and mental symptoms of menopause.

4. Provide basic information to the client on perimenopause or menopause and/or provide reading material on the subject (e.g., web sites like www.healthywomen.org).

5. Educate the client on factors that make earlier menopause more likely (e.g., higher body mass index, smoking, lack of physical activity, lower socioeconomic status).

3. Implement at least two strategies to help reduce hot flashes. (6, 7)

6. If the client is experiencing hot flashes, have her keep a diary to track when they happen; use this information to help determine associated triggers.

7. Explore options (e.g., supplements/herbs, oral contraceptives, HRT) for reducing hot flashes, which can adversely affect sleep and performing daily tasks.

4. Implement at least two strategies to relieve insomnia. (8, 9)

8. Educate the client on the relationship between insomnia/loss of sleep and its impact on overall cognitive functioning (e.g., concentration, memory, clarity of thought) and emotional functioning (e.g., irritability, depressive symptoms).

9. Encourage the client to implement new sleep induction habits (e.g., exercise early in the day, take a warm bath before retiring, drink chamomile tea, read, engage in meditation/yoga).

5. Maintain regular gynecological checkups. (10)

6. Implement a healthy diet and exercise regimen. (11, 12, 13)

7. Manage stress associated with adjustment-to-life transitions occurring at time of menopause. (14, 15, 16, 17)

10. Encourage the client to obtain proper and frequent gynecological checks, especially if she has symptoms such as heavy bleeding, bleeding between periods, pain and/or prolonged periods, and/or pain with sexual intercourse.

11. Assist the client in planning an exercise/yoga/medication routine that will be beneficial in reducing depressive symptoms, anxiety, and stress, as well as the risks of osteoporosis, heart disease, and weight gain/body image issues associated with menopause.

12. Encourage the client to eat a healthy diet that is low in fat and cholesterol; moderate in total fat; high in fiber; high in fruits, vegetables, and whole-grain foods; and well-balanced in vitamins and minerals, including calcium.

13. Encourage the client to incorporate the diet and exercise strategies into daily practice; discuss associated challenges and explore ways to overcome challenges.

14. Explore the sources of stress in the client's life (e.g., career change, return to school, caring for aging parent, balancing life responsibilities); process coping strategies and problem solving.

15. Facilitate a reduction in the client's self-perceived stress level by teaching her deep-breathing exercises, relaxation techniques, or guided imagery.

16. Help the client find new ways to bolster existing sources of social support (e.g., reach out to participate in planned activities, join new social groups).

17. Suggest that the client participate in off- and online support groups with other women who experience similar menopausal issues (e.g., hysterectomy, HRT choices, disruptive symptoms).

8. Identify the influence of sociocultural messages regarding menopause and their relationship to self-esteem. (18, 19)

18. Explore the relationship between sociocultural messages related to aging of the body or loss of reproductive function and the client's midlife self-concept.

19. Encourage the client to separate her personal experience of menopause from negative societal messages and the influence of those that are close to her.

9. Verbalize a more individualized and positive outlook on perimenopause and menopause. (20, 21, 22, 23)

20. Review the ways that having a strictly biological emphasis on menopause can lead to a view that the client's experience is predominated by illness and/or medical intervention (e.g., hormones, hysterectomy).

21. Challenge the client's internalized negative stereotypes about women and aging.

22. Formulate, along with the client, alternative ways of viewing menopause that do not include the typical message of deficiency or decline; use cognitive-restructuring techniques to assist the client in reframing negative attitudes toward menopause and aging and to eliminate catastrophizing self-statements.

23. Help the client reframe the negativity associated with perimenopause and menopause as times when a woman has achieved much in her life and is wise and experienced.

10. Differentiate between which midlife symptoms are due to perimenopause/ menopause and which may simply be concurrent developmental changes. (4, 10, 24)

4. Provide basic information to the client on perimenopause or menopause and/or provide reading material on the subject (e.g., web sites like www.healthywomen.org).

10. Encourage the client to obtain proper and frequent gynecological checks, especially if she has symptoms such as heavy bleeding, bleeding between periods, pain and/or prolonged periods, and/or pain with sexual intercourse.

24. Help the client differentiate between symptoms associated with perimenopause or menopause and those associated with concurrent developmental changes (e.g., changes in employment, family transitions, care for aging parents).

11. Define/redefine self as a sexual being in midlife; make adaptations to newly perceived roles. (25, 26)

25. Explore changes in the client's sexual activity and identify and address potential contributing factors (e.g., decreased sexual desire, depression, dyspareunia, decreased vaginal secretions, body image concerns).

26. Refer the client to read books such as *The Wisdom of Menopause* by Northrup, *The Sexy Years* by Somers, and a book of essays called *The Ageless Spirit: Reflections on Living Life to the Fullest in*

Midlife and the Years Beyond by Goldman.

12. Communicate openly with partner and develop a renewed sense of intimacy. (27)

27. Help the client to facilitate open communication and a renewed sense of intimacy with her partner; refer the client to couples counseling, if indicated.

13. Verbalize the process and outcome of one's self-reassessment and the positive implications for the future. (28)

28. Discuss with the client her process of self-assessment and reexamination and the positive implications for the future (e.g., achieved more experience, competence, and greater freedom).

—. _____ —. _____

_____ _____

—. _____ —. _____

_____ _____

—. _____ —. _____

_____ _____

DIAGNOSTIC SUGGESTIONS:

Axis I:	296.xx	Major Depressive Disorder
	300.02	Generalized Anxiety Disorder
	300.4	Dysthymic Disorder
	309.28	Adjustment Disorder with Mixed Anxiety and Depressed Mood
	302.71	Hypoactive Sexual Desire Disorder
	307.42	Primary Insomnia
	780.59	Breathing-Related Sleep Disorder
	V61.9	Relational Problem Related to Perimenopause or Menopause
	_____	_____
	_____	_____
Axis II:	V71.09	No Diagnosis
	799.9	Diagnosis Deferred
	_____	_____
	_____	_____

PARTNER RELATIONAL PROBLEMS

BEHAVIORAL DEFINITIONS

1. Experiences dissatisfaction, frustration, and hopelessness with regard to partner relationship.
2. Reports frequent arguments with partner.
3. Describes poor communication with partner.
4. Experiences verbal and/or physical abuse in a partner relationship.
5. Describes a lack of connection with partner, infrequent or no affection, and excessive involvement in activities outside of the relationship to avoid closeness to partner.
6. Verbalizes frustration and conflict in the partner relationship due to an imbalance in roles and responsibilities (e.g., childcare, home maintenance, work).
7. Reports discrimination, prejudice, or rejection from others due to an interracial or same-sex relationship.

—. _____
_____

—. _____
_____

—. _____
_____

LONG-TERM GOALS

1. Develop the necessary skills for effective, open communication and mutually satisfying intimacy.
2. Increase awareness of own role in relationship conflicts.
3. Develop a sense of own personal power and self-esteem within the relationship.

4. Commit to improve relationship by working together as a team.
5. Learn to identify escalating behaviors that lead to abuse.
6. Accept the termination of the relationship.

—. _____
_____
_____

—. _____
_____
_____

—. _____
_____

SHORT-TERM OBJECTIVES

THERAPEUTIC INTERVENTIONS

1. Attend and actively participate in conjoint sessions with the partner. (1, 2, 3)

1. Facilitate conjoint sessions that focus on increasing the couple's communication and problem-solving skills; acknowledge the frustration and anxiety with the state of the relationship.

2. Explore, along with the client, ongoing conflicts existent in the relationship, including physical abuse; if physical abuse is present, refer the client to appropriate resources to establish a safety plan and terminate conjoint sessions (see Domestic Violence/Battery chapter in this *Planner*).

3. Assist the client in identifying the positive behaviors that focus on relationship building.

2. Identify the positive aspects of the relationship. (3)

3. Assist the client in identifying the positive behaviors that focus on relationship building.

3. Each partner identifies her/his own role in the conflicts. (4, 5)

4. Assign the couple a between-sessions task recording in journals the positive and negative

things about the significant other and the relationship (or assign "Positive and Negative Contributions to the Relationship: Mine and Yours" in the *Adult Psychotherapy Homework Planner*, 2nd ed. by Jongsma); ask the couple not to show their journal material to each other until the next session, when the material will be processed.

5. Discuss the role of each partner for projection of and avoidance of responsibility for conflicts within the relationship.

4. Each partner commits to attempt to modify at least two specific behaviors that have been identified by self or the partner. (6, 7)

6. Assign each partner to list changes she/he needs to make as well as changes the other needs to make to improve the relationship (or assign "How Can We Meet Each Other's Needs" in the *Adult Psychotherapy Homework Planner*, 2nd ed. by Jongsma); process the list in conjoint sessions.

7. Seek a commitment from each partner to begin to work on changing specific behaviors on her/his list and on the list of the partner for her/him.

5. Increase the frequency and quality of communication with the partner. (8, 9, 10)

8. Assist the couple in identifying conflicts that can be addressed using communication, conflict-resolution, and/or problem-solving skills (see "Behavioral Marital Therapy" by Holzworth-Munroe and Jacobson in the *Handbook of Family Therapy*, 2nd ed. by Gurman and Knickerson [Eds.]).

9. Assign the couple to set aside daily 15 minutes that are

distraction free during which they can communicate about nonconflictual issues; practice during the therapy session, assisting each partner in clarifying communication and expression of feelings.

10. Encourage the couple to attend a communications skills-based relationship seminar; encourage them to continue to practice the skills obtained there.

6. Express thoughts and feelings regarding the relationship in a direct manner. (11, 12)

11. Teach the couple to reframe complaints into requests and to seek agreement from the partner to meet these requests.

12. Teach the client assertiveness or refer her to a group that will educate and facilitate assertiveness skills (see Low Self-Esteem/Lack of Assertiveness chapter in this *Planner*).

7. Both partners identify and verbalize at least three expectations for the relationship. (13, 14)

13. Validate the client's disappointment and disillusionment with the current relationship; assist the client with expressing her expectations and hopes regarding the relationship.

14. Confront unrealistic expectations regarding relationships, and assist the couple in adopting more realistic beliefs and expectations of each other and of the relationship.

8. Utilize at least two new conflict-resolution techniques to resolve issues reasonably. (15, 16, 17)

15. Teach the couple conflict-resolution techniques such as "Do's & Don't's List" and "Fair Fighting Steps" in *The Intimate Enemy: How to Fight Fair in Love and Marriage* by Bach and

Wyden; encourage the couple to practice these techniques in session and at home.

16. Use behavioral techniques (e.g., education, modeling, role-playing, corrective feedback, positive reinforcement) to teach the couple problem-solving and conflict-resolution skills, including defining the problem constructively and specifically, brainstorming options, compromise, choosing options, implementing a plan, and evaluating the results.

17. Assign the couple a homework exercise to use and record newly learned problem-solving and conflict-resolution skills (or assign "Applying Problem-Solving to Interpersonal Conflict" in the *Adult Psychotherapy Homework Planner,* 2nd ed. by Jongsma); process the results in session.

9. Identify a pattern of repeatedly forming destructive intimate relationships. (18)

18. Explore the family-of-origin history of each partner to discover patterns of destructive intimate relationship interactions that are being repeated in the present relationship; explore characteristics of a healthy relationship.

10. Both partners agree to a "time out" signal that either partner may give to stop interaction that may escalate into abuse. (19, 20, 21, 22)

19. Ask each partner to make a list of escalating behaviors that occur prior to abuse.

20. Assist the partners in identifying a clear verbal or behavioral signal to be used by either partner to terminate interaction immediately if either senses impending abuse.

21. Solicit a firm agreement from both partners that the "time out" signal will be responded to favorably without debate.

22. Assign implementation and recording the use of the "time out" signal and other conflict-resolution skills in daily interaction (or assign "Alternatives to Destructive Anger" in the *Adult Psychotherapy Homework Planner,* 2nd ed. by Jongsma).

11. Acknowledge the connection between substance abuse and the conflicts present within the relationship. (23)

23. Explore the role of substance abuse in precipitating conflict and/or abuse within the relationship.

12. The chemically dependent partner agrees to pursue treatment and seek a clean and sober lifestyle. (24)

24. Solicit an agreement for substance abuse treatment for the chemically dependent partner (see Chemical Dependence chapter in this *Planner*).

13. Identify the level of closeness/distance desired in a relationship and relate to fears of intimacy. (25, 26)

25. Assign the clients to read *Getting the Love You Want* by Hendrix and/or attend a workshop to create relationship skills.

26. Explore each partner's fears regarding intimacy and vulnerability to hurt, rejection, or abandonment.

14. Identify activities that are satisfying and enjoyable outside of the immediate relationship, including a social support system. (27)

27. Assist the client with identifying and engaging in satisfying activities outside of the immediate relationship.

15. Share family and childhood experiences with each other to increase understanding and empathy. (28)

28. Assign each client to complete a genogram; process each genogram in a conjoint session to promote greater empathy and awareness concerning each other.

16. Increase time spent in enjoyable contact with the partner. (29)

29. Assist the client in working with the partner to identify and plan rewarding social/recreational activities that can be shared with the partner (or assign "Identify and Schedule Pleasant Activities" in the *Adult Psychotherapy Homework Planner,* 2nd ed. by Jongsma).

17. Initiate verbal and physical affection behaviors with the partner. (30)

30. Explore and process any resistance surrounding initiating or receiving affection or sexual interactions with the partner.

18. Commit to the establishment of healthy, mutually satisfying sexual attitudes and behavior that is not a reflection of destructive earlier experiences. (31, 32)

31. Assist the client in exploring her sexual behavior, patterns, and beliefs.

32. Assist each partner in committing to develop healthy, mutually satisfying sexual beliefs, attitudes, and behavior that are independent of previous childhood, personal, or familial experiences (or assign "Factors Influencing Negative Sexual Attitudes" in the *Adult Psychotherapy Homework Planner,* 2nd ed. by Jongsma).

19. Verbalize the feelings associated with grieving the loss of the relationship. (33, 34, 35)

33. Assist the client with processing feelings associated with loss of the relationship.

34. Refer the client to a support group or divorce seminar to assist in resolving the loss and adjusting to a new life.

35. Assign the client to read *How to Survive the Loss of a Love* by Colgrove, Bloomfield, and McWilliams or *Surviving Separation and Divorce* by Oberlin); process key concepts.

20. Identify and replace negative attitudes (e.g., shame)

36. Explore with the client feelings, beliefs, and attitudes related to

associated with being a single female. (36, 37)

being a separated, divorced, and/or single woman; discuss the impact of gender role socialization on such beliefs and attitudes.

37. Help and encourage the client in hcr adjustmcnt to living alone and being single; challenge unrealistic beliefs regarding her self-worth and attractiveness.

21. Verbalize plans as to how to cope with potential loneliness. (38, 39)

38. Direct the client to resources and social opportunities within the community; assist the client in integrating these resources into a plan to start building new social relationships.

39. Assist the client with identifying satisfying activities; assign engagement in these activities and process the experience.

—. _____   —. _____

   _____   _____

—. _____   —. _____

   _____   _____

—. _____   —. _____

   _____   _____

DIAGNOSTIC SUGGESTIONS:

Axis I: 309.0   Adjustment Disorder with Depressed Mood
              309.24   Adjustment Disorder with Anxiety
              V61.1   Partner Relational Problem
              309.81   Posttraumatic Stress Disorder

              _____   _____

              _____   _____

Axis II: V71.09   No Diagnosis
                  799.9   Diagnosis Deferred

_____   _____

_____   _____

POSTPARTUM MOOD DISORDERS (PPD)

Chapter co-authored with Wendy Heath-Gainer, EdS

BEHAVIORAL DEFINITIONS

1. Demonstrates signs of depressed mood, hopelessness, low self-esteem, irritability, and loss of interest in usual activities within the first three months to one year after childbirth.
2. Evidences sleep disturbance, fatigue, and loss of appetite within the first three months to one year after childbirth.
3. Possesses feelings of negativity or ambivalence towards infant, as well as expression of guilt, concern, or doubt about ability to care for child.
4. Displays symptoms of Generalized Anxiety Disorder, Obsessive-Compulsive Disorder, and/or Panic Disorder after giving birth to a child.
5. Presents with intrusive, obsessive ruminations regarding her infant's well-being, possibly involving thoughts of committing some violent act against the child.
6. Expresses distress regarding losses of identity, independence, autonomy, and paid employment subsequent to childbirth.
7. Verbalizes a lack of validation for feelings and behavior within a supportive interpersonal relationship and cultural context.
8. Experiences symptoms of depression related to lack of or limited social support, childcare stressors, inequitable division of household labor, and social isolation.
9. Verbalizes recurrent thoughts of death or suicidal ideation.
10. Feels the need to commit or actually commits infanticide due to postpartum psychosis (e.g., command hallucinations to kill the baby or delusions such as a belief that the baby is devil-possessed).

—. _____

_____

—. _____

_____

—. _____

_____

LONG-TERM GOALS

1. Reduce the signs and symptoms related to depression and anxiety.
2. Reduce childcare stressors via utilization of available resources (e.g., family, friends, neighbors, community resources).
3. Develop an increased sense of self-efficacy regarding childrearing, revised roles, and new identity.
4. Develop a positive relationship with and feelings toward the infant.
5. Negotiate with the partner to meet the basic responsibilities of childcare, work, relationship, and family in a mutually agreeable manner.
6. Develop a social support network and participate in nurturing activities on a regular basis.

—. _____

_____

—. _____

_____

—. _____

_____

SHORT-TERM OBJECTIVES	THERAPEUTIC INTERVENTIONS
1. Verbalize symptoms that may contribute to current condition. (1)	1. Explore with the client the symptoms of mood disorder as well as time, situation, and frequency of occurrence, identifying precipitating events, thoughts, feelings, and behavior that she is currently experiencing; isolate potential causes and contributors.
2. Cooperate with psychological testing to obtain a quantifiable measure of the existence and	2. Administer standardized psychometric measure of PPD to the client (e.g., Postpartum

severity of the postpartum mood disorder (PPD). (2)

Depression Screening Scale [PDSS]); combine results with interview data to obtain a complete picture of the client's situation and review the results with the client.

3. Participate in a physician evaluation to detect potential medical conditions contributing to current mood disorder. (3)

3. Refer the client to a physician to address potential hormone imbalances and to rule out any medical cause for her mood disturbance (e.g., thyroid dysfunction, anemia); if necessary, refer the client to a psychiatrist for an evaluation for appropriate psychotropic medication.

4. Recount possible traumatic aspects of childbirth; describe how this has affected current feelings of depression, anxiety, and stress. (4, 5)

4. Explore whether the client had an adverse childbirth experience that may contribute to current depression and anxiety; ask open and nonthreatening questions regarding the birth.

5. Provide attentive listening and acceptance of the client's perspective; encourage the client to tell her unique story, while using reflective listening skills.

5. Establish the amount of sleep needed per night; implement strategies devised to maximize rest time. (6, 7)

6. Discuss ways to minimize the client's sleep deprivation (e.g., implement demand feedings rather than scheduled feedings if breast-feeding; enlist a family member or hire a babysitter so mother can catch up on sleep).

7. Assist the client in regulating her baby's sleep habits in order to make the client's rest times more predictable (e.g., recommend *Healthy Sleep Habits, Happy Child* by Weissbluth).

6. Verbalize an understanding of the connection between mood

8. Explore with the client her understanding of her symptoms

disorder symptoms and significant life changes. (8, 9, 10)

(e.g., sleep disturbance, childcare stressors, social isolation, lack of social support, and hormonal shifts) and their origins; use the discussion to gauge her psychoeducational needs.

9. Provide the client with an overview of current knowledge regarding her symptoms and their potential causes, including the role of hormonal changes, sleep deprivation, and psychological stress of new motherhood; share with her the fact that 60% to 80% of women experience mood fluctuations shortly after childbirth.

10. Refer the client to sources that will extend her knowledge in the area of PPD and effective strategies (e.g., *Depression in New Mothers: Causes, Consequences, and Treatment Alternatives* by Kendall-Tackett; *Postpartum Survival Guide* by Dunnewold and Sanford).

7. Reduce self-pressure to do all of the childcare; and if returning to work, only take on what is manageable, if possible, until adjustment to motherhood is made. (11, 12)

11. Discuss with the client the realities of multiple roles and responsibilities; challenge unrealistic thinking (e.g., "I should be able to do everything perfectly on my own").

12. Explore and role-play, along with the client, approaches to balancing multiple roles, including talking to her boss about flexibility on the job and negotiating with partner/family members for assistance.

8. Articulate feelings about pregnancy, motherhood, and the baby. (13, 14)

13. Explore the client's feelings and attitudes toward pregnancy, motherhood, and the baby.

14. Encourage the client's expression of feelings (e.g., isolation, hopelessness) by utilizing open questions; validate her feelings regarding childrearing, revised roles, and new identity.

9. Articulate feelings associated with PPD. (14, 15)

14. Encourage the client's expression of feelings (e.g., isolation, hopelessness) by utilizing open questions; validate her feelings regarding childrearing, revised roles, and new identity.

15. Teach the client to counter defeatist self-statements regarding postpartum mood symptoms (e.g., replace "I am ashamed and embarrassed that I have PPD" with "What I am feeling are symptoms of this illness; I am not making this up"; or "I can snap out of this if I try harder" to "I can choose to be active in the course of my recovery and help myself feel better").

10. Replace negative thoughts about self with more positive, constructive thoughts. (16)

16. Explore and challenge the client's distorted thinking that has contributed to feelings of inadequacy or self-blame (e.g., "I should always enjoy being a mother"; "If I ask for help, then people will think that I can't do any of this by myself"; "If I decide to do something just for myself, then I am selfish").

11. Identify personal indicators of competence and strength. (17)

17. Affirm the client's competence by highlighting her accomplishments and identifying her strengths.

12. Openly express concerns to partner regarding division of

18. Explore the client's level of satisfaction with her partner's

labor and need for emotional support. (18, 19)

participation in childcare, household chores, and provision of emotional support.

19. Role-play with the client effective approaches to communicating with her partner; engage or refer the client and her partner to couples counseling to increase her support.

13. Connect with other mothers at least once per week to discuss issues such as nursing, and balancing multiple roles. (20)

20. Encourage the client to identify and develop relationships with other mothers (e.g., involvement with neighborhood playgroups, attend "Mommy and Me" support group, attend a PPD support group, Internet sites such as Postpartum Support International at www.postpartum.net/brief.html).

14. Engage in self-nurturing activities at least two times per week. (21)

21. Explore, along with the client, self-nurturing activities (e.g., reading, exercising, healthy eating, taking a bath, meditating), and encourage her to pursue these activities on a regular schedule.

15. Nurture healthy relationships with existing friends, and cultivate new social contacts. (22, 23)

22. Explore the client's social network, and encourage her to participate in external social contacts on a regular basis.

23. Assist the client in identifying three ways to increase her social contacts (e.g., taking a class, joining a church group, forming a group of young mothers within neighborhood).

16. Comply with counselor and medical doctor's interventions for the well- being of self and baby. (24)

24. In rare cases, intervene assertively with treatment of the client's psychotic symptoms (e.g., immediate psychiatric hospitalization), as well as ensuring the safety of her infant.

——. _____   ——. _____
   _____   _____
——. _____   ——. _____
   _____   _____
——. _____   ——. _____
   _____   _____

DIAGNOSTIC SUGGESTIONS:

Axis I: 296.xx   Major Depressive Disorder with Postpartum
                        Onset
               296.xx   Bipolar I Disorder with Postpartum Onset
               296.89   Bipolar II Disorder with Postpartum Onset
               298.8   Brief Psychotic Disorder with Postpartum Onset

               _____ _____
               _____ _____

Axis II: V71.09   No Diagnosis
               799.9   Diagnosis Deferred

               _____ _____
               _____ _____

SEXUAL ABUSE (CHILDHOOD)

Chapter co-authored with Anneliese A. Singh, MS and Danica G. Hays, PhD

BEHAVIORAL DEFINITIONS

1. Reports having experienced childhood sexual abuse.
2. Reports a family environment where primary caregivers were neglectful, abusive, and/or distracted (e.g., substance abuse, socially isolated, domestic violence, alternate caregivers, blended family, mental illness).
3. Describes an unstable community environment during childhood (e.g., poverty, exposure to discrimination, low social support and resources).
4. Demonstrates hyperarousal symptoms (e.g., easily startled, panic, sleep disturbance) associated with emotional distress (e.g., extreme emotional expression, irritability).
5. Presents with intrusive symptoms (e.g., flashbacks, dissociation) that disrupt day-to-day functioning at work, home, and social settings.
6. Presents with avoidance strategies utilized to suppress traumatic memories and cope with emotional pain (e.g., substance abuse, suicidal ideation, self-injurious behavior).
7. Verbalizes a negative self-concept associated with the sexual abuse experience (e.g., self-blame, guilt, low self-esteem, powerlessness).
8. Demonstrates difficulty in interpersonal relationships stemming from abuse history (e.g., boundary confusion, domestic violence, distrust, emotional numbing).

—. _____
_____
—. _____
_____
—. _____
_____

LONG-TERM GOALS

1. Develop insight into how childhood sexual abuse has impacted self-concept, sexuality, resilience, and view of the world and relationships.
2. Reduce emotional, physical, and/or sexual distress experienced as a result of childhood sexual abuse.
3. Reclaim self-esteem, security, and personal power that were restricted in an abusive and/or neglectful family environment.
4. Reduce victimization identity, resolving thoughts and feelings about the abuser(s) and other family relationships.
5. Develop healthy relationships where a wide range of emotions and personal safety are experienced.

—. _____
_____

—. _____
_____

—. _____
_____

SHORT-TERM OBJECTIVES

1. Describe the trauma story within the family and community environment; articulate the nature, frequency, and duration of the abuse. (1, 2, 3, 4)

THERAPEUTIC INTERVENTIONS

1. Cultivate a safe, trusting therapeutic environment through verbal and nonverbal displays of unconditional positive regard, warmth, empathy, and acceptance toward the client.

2. Explore the client's history of sexual abuse, gathering the data patiently and sensitively.

3. Gather information about family and community constellation, including dysfunction and/or intergenerational trauma; construct a family genogram and/or assign a gender and cultural role exploration exercise.

2. Articulate any present suicide ideation, plan, and/or intent, or self-injurious behavior, as well as any history of suicidal thoughts and/or gestures. (5, 6)

3. Identify a support system of individuals who will be encouraging and helpful in aiding the recovery process. (7, 8)

4. Articulate symptoms of hyperarousal, intrusion, and avoidance. (9, 10, 11, 12)

4. Facilitate understanding of the client's roles and responsibilities within the family and community environment and associated thoughts and feelings before, during, and after the abuse.

5. Assess the client's current level of risk for suicide, exploring any previous suicide attempts; reduce risk for suicide by removing access and engaging in a safety contract.

6. Arrange for hospitalization, as necessary, when the client is judged to be harmful to self.

7. Review the client's social network with the goal of identifying those individuals who would be compassionate and encourage her to enlist their support.

8. Encourage the client to attend a support group for survivors of sexual abuse.

9. Assess the client for current and historical experience of hyper-arousal symptoms (e.g., startle response, panic, sleep disturb-ance) and intense emotionality.

10. Validate the client's intense emotions that arise when describing the trauma experience and introduce affect regulation techniques (e.g., deep breathing, self-awareness).

11. Assess the client's current and historical experience of intrusive symptoms (e.g., dissociation, flashbacks); normalize intrusive symptoms as necessary coping tools used to survive sexual

trauma while encouraging the client's reality orientation.

12. Identify the client's current and historical instances of triggers related to the use of avoidance strategies (e.g., addiction to substances, food, relationships) and explore their relationship to the sexual trauma.

5. Acknowledge the connection between emotional and behavioral symptoms and the childhood trauma. (13, 14)

13. Assist the client in gaining insight into the relationship between hyperarousal, intrusive, and/or avoidance symptoms and the childhood trauma as maladaptive coping responses.

14. Provide psychoeducational information that explains to the client the fight-or-flight response that survivors utilize in an attempt to heal from sexual abuse.

6. Identify avoidance strategies that disrupt current functioning and implement healthy, alternative coping responses. (12, 15, 16, 17)

12. Identify the client's current and historical instances of triggers related to the use of avoidance strategies (e.g., addiction to substances, food, relationships) and explore their relationship to the sexual trauma.

15. Educate the client about the importance of developing and maintaining daily healthy coping (e.g., eating, sleeping) during trauma work.

16. Assist the client in adopting alternate coping and resilience strategies that are healthy (e.g., utilization of support networks, self-education, social activism).

17. Teach the client stress management strategies (e.g., deep breathing, journaling of emotions) in order to increase her

7. Read at least one book on female survivors of childhood sexual trauma. (18)

18. Assign the client bibliotherapy resources detailing the shared experience of sexual trauma survivors (e.g., *The Courage to Heal* by Bass and Davis; *The Sexual Healing Journey* by Maltz; *Healing the Incest Wound* by Courtois).

healthy coping mechanisms and self-soothing capacities.

8. Decrease secrecy in the family by informing key nonabusive members regarding the abuse. (19, 20)

19. Hold conjoint sessions where the client tells her partner of the abuse.

20. Facilitate family sessions with the client, assisting and supporting her in revealing the abuse to family members.

9. Identify negative thoughts and feelings about self related to the abuse experience. (21, 22, 23, 24)

21. Assess the relationship between the client's cultural background and/or gender and internalized negative messages related to shame and guilt about the abuse experience.

22. Explore and identify the client's distorted, negative automatic thoughts associated with the sexual abuse.

23. Assist the client in developing positive, reality-based messages for self to replace the distorted, negative self-talk.

24. Assign the client homework focusing on the ways that sexual trauma has shaped her self-concept in negative ways (e.g., "Changing from Victim to Survivor" or "Replacing Fears with Positive Messages" in the *Adult Psychotherapy Homework Planner,* 2nd ed. by Jongsma).

10. Understand powerlessness experienced during abuse and

25. Validate the client's feelings of powerlessness experienced during

increase sense of personal power. (25, 26, 27, 28)

the abuse and assist her in transferring blame from herself to the perpetrator; confront and process with the client any statements that reflect her taking responsibility for the abuse.

26. Assign homework activities to increase the client's personal power and self-esteem (e.g., defense class, self-care activities); encourage and support areas of the client's life where she experiences internal strength.

27. Introduce stories of strong female role models who have survived sexual abuse (e.g., Oprah Winfrey, Maya Angelou, Trudie Scales).

28. Assign the client to complete a list of resilience strategies used to manage historical and current pain of abuse (e.g., social skills, problem-solving skills, internal locus of control, self-efficacy).

11. Identify at least three victimization patterns related to trauma story. (29)

29. Explore and identify relationship patterns that decrease self-esteem and assertion of emotional, physical, and sexual needs.

12. List uncomfortable or challenging emotions and increase their expression. (30, 31, 32)

30. Identify the client's numbing of difficult emotions (e.g., anger, fear, sadness, pleasure) that are experienced in relation to the sharing of her trauma story.

31. Introduce a chart that lists different feelings to encourage and increase the client's ability to identify and regulate her challenging emotions.

32. Use role-play and behavioral rehearsal to encourage the client to express feelings that are triggered by various situations.

13. Report increased ability to demonstrate assertiveness in relationships. (33, 34)

33. Introduce assertiveness training (e.g., role-playing, empty-chair technique) in order to assist the client in identifying and reclaiming her personal needs; model assertive responses to current and past problems (e.g., using "I statements," honesty, clarification).

34. Assist the client in identifying historical and current cultural and gender norm barriers to developing assertiveness; encourage healthy assertive expression.

14. If physically safe, express feelings to and about the perpetrator, including the impact the abuse has had both at the time of occurrence and currently. (35, 36, 37)

35. Assign the client to write a letter to the perpetrator of the abuse; process the letter within the session, explaining that the letter does not necessarily need to be sent.

36. Guide the client in an empty-chair conversation exercise with a key figure connected to the abuse (e.g., perpetrator, sibling, or parent) telling them of the sexual abuse and its effects; explore potentially positive and negative consequences of disclosure.

37. Hold a conjoint session where the client confronts the perpetrator of the abuse (only if the client's ongoing safety is guaranteed); afterward, process her feelings and thoughts related to the experience.

15. Increase trust of self and others by taking a risk getting close to people. (38, 39)

38. Introduce to the client the idea that survivors use an "either/or" approach to trust in relationships; suggest that trust can be given in graduated steps.

39. Identify and suggest that the client take small calculated risks that have a good chance of success in relationships (e.g., asking a friend for comfort, seeking out a survivor support group).

16. Verbalize an increased awareness of healthy and unhealthy boundary-settings in personal relationships and demonstrate an increased ability to set healthy boundaries. (40, 41, 42)

40. Assign the client to read materials on setting limits with her family-of-origin, intimate partnerships, and other relationships (e.g., *Boundaries: Where You End and I Begin* by Katherine; *Safe People* by Cloud and Townsend).

41. Assign the client to complete a personal bill of rights that lists her physical, psychological, and sexual boundaries.

42. Review instances where the client has had to set boundaries in relationships; reinforce success and redirect for failure.

17. Articulate at least 10 personal positive qualities and recognize importance of fostering self-esteem. (43, 44)

43. Utilize cognitive reframing to increase the clients' internalized positive messages about herself.

44. Assist the client in identifying specific positive qualities that she would like to think and feel about herself (or assign "Positive Self-Talk" or "Acknowledging My Strengths" in the *Adult Psychotherapy Homework Planner*, 2nd ed. by Jongsma).

18. Engage in at least two enjoyable wellness or self-care activities (e.g., walking, stress management, hobbies). (45)

45. Introduce psychoeducation on wellness and self-care, and encourage goal-setting for daily wellness and self-care activities (or assign "Identify and Schedule Pleasant Activities" in the *Adult Psychotherapy Homework Planner*, 2nd ed. by Jongsma).

—. _____   —. _____
   _____   _____
—. _____   —. _____
   _____   _____
—. _____   —. _____
   _____   _____

DIAGNOSTIC SUGGESTIONS:

Axis I: 300.4   Dysthymic Disorder
               296.xx   Major Depressive Disorder
               300.02   Generalized Anxiety Disorder
               309.81   Posttraumatic Stress Disorder
               300.14   Dissociative Identity Disorder
               303.90   Alcohol Dependence
               304.80   Polysubstance Dependence
               995.53   Sexual Abuse of Child, Victim
               995.83   Sexual Abuse of Adult, Victim

               _____ _____
               _____ _____

Axis II: 301.82   Avoidant Personality Disorder
               301.83   Borderline Personality Disorder
               301.6   Dependent Personality Disorder
               V71.09   No Diagnosis
               799.9   Diagnosis Deferred

               _____ _____
               _____ _____

SEXUAL ASSAULT AND RAPE

Chapter co-authored with Anneliese A. Singh, MS

BEHAVIORAL DEFINITIONS

1. Reports assault of a sexual nature by an offender in her personal network.
2. Reports assault of a sexual nature by a stranger.
3. Describes feelings of confusion, shock, anxiety, denial, and/or numbness.
4. Presents with intrusive symptoms (e.g., flashbacks, dissociation) related to the sexual assault that disrupts day-to-day functioning at work, home, and social settings.
5. Describes hyperarousal symptoms (e.g., easily startled, panic symptoms, sleep disturbance) associated with emotional distress (e.g., extreme emotional expression, irritability) related to sexual assault.
6. Presents with avoidance strategies related to the sexual assault utilized to cope with emotional pain (e.g., substance abuse, suicidal ideation, self-injurious behavior, social withdrawal).
7. Demonstrates negative self-concept associated with the sexual assault (e.g., self-blame, guilt, powerlessness).

___. _____
_____

___. _____
_____

___. _____
_____

LONG-TERM GOALS

1. Establish and maintain physical safety.
2. Reduce victimization identity; shift from self-blame to placing responsibility for the sexual assault on the offender.
3. Improve emotional and cognitive functioning so that the sexual assault is not the primary focus of life, but a part of one's history.
4. Reclaim self-esteem, security, and personal power that were restricted as a result of the sexual assault.
5. Develop healthy and caring relationships where a wide range of emotions and personal safety can be experienced.

—. _____
   _____
   _____
—. _____
   _____
   _____
—. _____
   _____

SHORT-TERM OBJECTIVES	THERAPEUTIC INTERVENTIONS
1. Describe the experience of sexual assault and related thoughts and feelings. (1)	1. Cultivate a safe, trusting therapeutic environment through verbal and nonverbal displays of unconditional positive regard, warmth, empathy, and acceptance of the client as she tells her story or sexual assault.
2. Cooperate with referral to medical/legal resources. (2)	2. Refer the client for medical treatment and/or legal resources as necessary.
3. Describe the perception of negative and/or positive consequences of reporting the sexual assault to authorities and to friends or family. (3)	3. Explore with the client the potential implications of reporting sexual assault to authorities and family and/or friends.

4. Identify a network of supportive and validating people and helpful resources during recovery from sexual assault. (4)

5. Articulate any suicidal ideation and/or self-injurious behavior (including intent, plan, and means). (5, 6, 7)

6. Describe hyperarousal, intrusion, and avoidance symptoms associated with the sexual assault. (8, 9, 10)

7. Articulate trauma history as a child, adolescent, or adult (11)

4. Review the client's social network with the goal of identifying individuals who will support the survivor's recovery from the assault.

5. Assess and explore current and past suicidal ideation and/or self-injurious behavior (i.e., intent, plan, means) and have the client sign a safety contract if necessary.

6. Notify the client's family and significant others of her suicidal ideation; ask them to form a 24-hour suicide watch until the crisis subsides.

7. Arrange for hospitalization when the client is judged to be uncontrollably harmful to self.

8. Actively assess current and historical instances of hyperarousal, intrusion, and avoidance symptoms.

9. Validate and normalize hyperarousal, intrusion, and avoidance symptoms and link them to the client's experience of sexual assault.

10. Provide psychoeducation on the psychological and physical impacts of sexual assault.

11. Explore the client's trauma history (e.g., emotional, physical, sexual, natural disasters, other unresolved trauma) and the cultural context of this history (e.g., race/ethnicity, religious/ spiritual affiliation, gender, etc.); relate this to current functioning.

8. Verbalize the various aspects of the sexual assault experience and its impact on emotional, cognitive, and/or spiritual functioning, including feelings of powerlessness and anger. (10, 12, 13, 14)

10. Provide psychoeducation on the psychological and physical impacts of sexual assault.

12. Explore the client's account of the sexual assault (i.e., nature, frequency, and duration of assault), ensuring that the client determines the level of detail provided.

13. Validate and normalize the client's reactions to the sexual assault experience.

14. Introduce psychoeducation on distorted cognitions and the importance of reframing the sexual assault experience as a step in the recovery process (e.g., placing blame only on the assailant).

9. Articulate the stages of recovery from sexual assault and related grieving process, identifying the current stage. (15)

15. Provide psychoeducation on the stages of trauma and associated grief (e.g., shock, denial, impact/acceptance).

10. Read and/or listen to material that articulates the common thoughts and feelings after sexual assault to increase understanding of how one is impacted by these reactions. (16, 17, 18)

16. Assign bibliotherapy resources detailing the common thoughts and feelings (e.g., self-blame, worthlessness, fear) of sexual assault survivors (e.g., *The Rape Recovery Handbook: Step-By-Step Help for Survivors of Sexual Assault* by Matsakis; *The Sexual Healing Journey* by Maltz).

17. Ask the client to make a list of the psychological, physical, and/or spiritual impacts of sexual assault.

18. Provide information on the range of emotions that are healthy for the client to experience (e.g., happiness, sadness, fear, anger).

11. Identify ways that the offender restricted or limited the client's power and link to at least three victimization cognitions/patterns. (13, 19)

13. Validate and normalize the client's reactions to the sexual assault experience.

19. Explore with the client how her power and sense of control were limited or restricted by the offender and the assault experience; link the offender actions to her victimization cognitions.

12. Eliminate verbalizations of self-blame and place blame on the offender. (20, 21)

20. Assess the client's tendency to blame herself for the assault and related cognitive distortions (e.g., "I am responsible for the assault by walking or dressing provocatively"); explore familial, societal, and cultural sources of self-blame.

21. Assist the client in replacing her cognitive distortions with realistic thinking.

13. Journal and/or write a letter to the offender about issues of safety, self-blame, worthlessness, guilt, and/or powerlessness. (22)

22. Assign the client to write a letter to the offender (that she will not necessarily send) expressing her thoughts and feelings about the sexual assault; understand that expressions of appropriate anger are culturally influenced.

14. Read at least one book on boundary-setting and safety. (23)

23. Assign the client to read materials on boundary-setting and safety (e.g., *Boundaries: Where You End and I Begin* by Katherine, *Boundaries in Dating* by Cloud and Townsend; *Boundaries in Marriage* by Cloud and Townsend); discuss the client's reactions to the material and reinforce appropriate boundary-setting.

15. Identify at least three sources of personal power in one's life. (24)

24. Ask the client to make a list of coping and resilience strategies before and after the sexual assault

(e.g., sense of personal control, self-efficacy, problem-solving skills).

16. Increase self-trust and trust of others by taking risks and getting close to people. (25, 26, 27)

25. Collaborate with the client to list ways she can safely create intimacy in her relationships with partners, family, and/or friends.

26. Hold conjoint session where the client tells her partner, spouse, family, and/or friend(s) who are safe and nonabusive about the sexual assault.

27. If the client has a partner or spouse, hold conjoint session to explore issues of trust, intimacy, and sexuality.

17. Engage in assertive behavior (e.g., emotional, physical, sexual) and set healthy boundaries in relationships. (28, 29)

28. Introduce stories of strong female role models, particularly those who share the cultural background of the client, who have survived sexual assault.

29. Refer the client to a workshop on self-defense, assertiveness, and/or empowerment.

18. Implement stress management and wellness strategies. (30, 31, 32, 33, 34)

30. Introduce psychoeducation on self-care and wellness, encouraging the client to engage in at least one therapeutic activity (e.g., art, music, dance, movement, culturally relevant ceremonies) as a way to decrease her feelings of anxiety and fear, as well as increase feelings of self-expression and self-empowerment.

31. Introduce stress management strategies in session (e.g., deep breathing, muscle relaxation, yoga, artistic expression, music).

32. Assess the client's reaction to stress management strategies for

dissociation, presence of fear, and loss of control.

33. Assign the client a behavioral chart to track her daily self-care strategies that are effective.

34. Assign stress management and wellness activities with people in the client's support network.

__. _____   __. _____

    _____   _____

__. _____   __. _____

    _____   _____

__. _____   __. _____

    _____   _____

DIAGNOSTIC SUGGESTIONS:

Axis I:	995.83	Sexual Abuse of Adult, Victim
	308.3	Acute Stress Disorder
	309.0	Adjustment Disorder with Depressed Mood
	309.24	Adjustment Disorder with Anxiety
	296.2x	Major Depressive Disorder, Single Episode
	300.4	Dysthymic Disorder
	311	Depressive Disorder NOS
	300.3	Obsessive-Compulsive Disorder
	300.02	Generalized Anxiety Disorder
	309.81	Posttraumatic Stress Disorder
	300.14	Dissociative Identity Disorder
	303.90	Alcohol Dependence
	304.80	Polysubstance Dependence
	_____	_____
	_____	_____

Axis II:	301.82	Avoidant Personality Disorder
	301.83	Borderline Personality Disorder
	301.50	Histrionic Personality Disorder
	301.6	Dependent Personality Disorder
	V71.09	No Diagnosis
	799.9	Diagnosis Deferred
	_____	_____
	_____	_____

SEXUALITY/ISSUES IN SEXUAL FUNCTIONING

Chapter co-authored with Ekta Aulakh, EdS

BEHAVIORAL DEFINITIONS

1. Experiences discomfort with own sexuality due to familial messages, religious values, or cultural norms.
2. Experiences discomfort and avoidance of sexual situations due to distorted internalized gender role stereotypes, poor body image, or confusion about sexual orientation or identity.
3. Demonstrates sexual aversion or inhibition due to physical, sexual, or emotional abuse.
4. Demonstrates sexual inhibition, avoidance, or distress due to partner betrayal, fear of partner, or negative communication patterns with partner.
5. Experiences distress or interpersonal difficulty due to inability to attain or maintain usual physiological response of sexual excitement (i.e., lubrication, swelling) or inability to experience orgasm.
6. Experiences genital pain before, during, or after sexual intercourse in spite of a desire to be in the sexual situation.
7. Avoids sexual activity or is unable to enjoy sex due to significant anxiety about contracting a sexually transmitted disease (STD) or other undesired consequences (e.g., pregnancy).
8. Experiences difficulty establishing dating boundaries, including using sexual protection due to lack of assertiveness, low self-esteem, or poor communication skills.

—. _____

_____

—. _____

_____

—. _____

_____

LONG-TERM GOALS

1. Experience comfort and satisfaction in sexual situations.
2. Experience enjoyment and lack of anxiety and/or distress during sexual activity.
3. Establish and verbalize healthy dating and sexual boundaries.
4. Demonstrate confidence and self-assuredness regarding one's sexuality.
5. Establish effective and healthy communication with partner regarding sexuality.

—. _____

_____

—. _____

_____

—. _____

_____

SHORT-TERM OBJECTIVES	THERAPEUTIC INTERVENTIONS
1. Verbalize past and current sexual functioning and satisfaction. (1, 2, 3)	1. Develop a safe, trusting therapeutic environment through displays of unconditional positive regard, empathy, and acceptance.
	2. Gather a complete sexual history from the client, including current sexual activity and functioning; sexual satisfaction; relationship history; effects of contraception, pregnancy, illness, medication, and aging on sexual response; history of presenting problem; substance abuse; and experiences of sexual or physical abuse.
	3. Offer hope and encouragement and help the client view her sexual problem as solvable.

2. Verbalize sexual beliefs, attitudes, and behaviors learned in family-of-origin and society. (4, 5, 6)

4. Explore the role of the client's experiences in her family-of-origin on her sexual beliefs, attitudes, and behaviors.

5. Explore the role of the client's religious training in influencing feelings of guilt and shame surrounding her sexual behavior and thoughts.

6. Explore the role of societal gender role messages on the client's sexual beliefs, attitudes, and behaviors.

3. Access information regarding human sexuality and health services. (7, 8, 9)

7. Assist the client with vocabulary to describe subjective or physical experience related to sexual ignorance.

8. Provide the client with information about human sexual biology and life-stage changes; refer the client to web sites such as the Sexuality Information and Education Council of the United States (http://siecus.org), Planned Parenthood (www.plannedparenthood .org/ sexual-health/ women-health.htm) and the Alan Guttmacher Institute (http:www.guttmacher.org).

9. Provide the client with information regarding services for contraception and abortion, STD prevention and treatment, and sexual trauma.

4. Describe thoughts and feelings regarding sexual relationships and dating norms. (10)

10. Explore the client's positive and negative thoughts and feelings in regard to her sexual relationships, dating norms, and contraceptive use.

5. Communicate feelings of anxiety regarding sexual acts or their possible consequences (e.g., pregnancy, sexually transmitted disease, loss of partner, loss of reputation). (11, 12)

11. Help the client verbalize fears associated with sexual activity; explore approaches to minimizing or avoiding possible negative consequences (e.g., condom usage, communication with partner).

12. Encourage the client to seek out literature and professionals in order to better understand perceived viable threats of sexual activity; refer the client to resources and services for contraception and STD prevention and treatment.

6. Verbalize feelings of sexual aversion, mistrust, or inhibition of sexual pleasure. (13, 14)

13. Discuss and assess the role of depression or anxiety in the client's inability to be aroused or find pleasure in sexual activity.

14. Explore the role of the client's past experiences of physical, sexual, or emotional abuse on her current sexual functioning.

7. Take prescribed medication for Sexual Arousal Disorder and report its effectiveness with sexual stimulation and any side effects. (15, 16)

15. Refer the client to a physician for a physical examination and possible medication.

16. Review medications taken by the client with regard to their impact on sexual interest and arousal and possible negative side effects.

8. Resolve trauma related to past physical, sexual, or emotional abuse; understand the connection between prior trauma and current sexual difficulties. (14, 17, 18)

14. Explore the role of the client's past experiences of physical, sexual, or emotional abuse on her current sexual functioning.

17. Resolve the client's feelings of guilt, blame, and shame; engage her in exercises that foster self-respect (see Sexual Abuse [Childhood] chapter in this *Planner* and *Healing the Trauma of Abuse* by Copeland and Harris).

9. Verbalize feelings related to sexual avoidance or distress due to perceived inability to meet cultural norms regarding correct or ideal sexuality. (19, 20, 21)

10. Develop positive thoughts and feelings towards one's sexuality. (22, 23, 24)

11. Verbalize comfort with own sexuality and affirm sexual rights. (25, 26, 27)

18. Use cognitive therapy techniques to resolve the client's distorted thoughts of guilt or shame related to abuse experiences.

19. Explore the client's anxiety and shame about her body and sexual attractiveness; assign body exploration and awareness exercises (e.g., *Sexual Awareness* by McCarthy and McCarthy).

20. Explore the client's confusion or shame about her sexual orientation or identity, or about sexual fantasies and desires.

21. Explore conflict between sexual norms of client's subculture or culture of origin and those of the dominant culture.

22. Engage in cognitive restructuring of the client's beliefs in regards to sexual activity and sexuality; identify and change irrational beliefs that interfere with enjoyable sexual experiences.

23. Ask the client to make a list of positive statements in regards to her body, body image, and/or sexual performance.

24. Validate the client's feelings and encourage her to assert her preferences in regard to sexual activity and her sexuality; respect the client's cultural values as they relate to sexuality.

25. Recommend that the client access resources related to understanding one's body and improving sexual activity (e.g., *For Yourself: The Fulfillment of Female Sexuality* by Barbach).

26. Assist the client in the development of self-esteem; engage in role-play to practice assertiveness.

27. Discuss with the client the right to sexual freedom (excluding all forms of sexual coercion, exploitation, and abuse), sexual autonomy and safety, sexual pleasure, and sexual information.

12. Explore one's sexuality through educational videos and books. (28, 29)

28. If religious views permit, encourage client to purchase educational videos of sexual activities to teach enhancement of fantasy, masturbation, and sexual behaviors (e.g., *Sex for One: The Joy of Self-Loving* by Dodson; *Better Sex Video Series: Volumes 1-3* by Sinclair Intimacy Institute).

29. Suggest that the client read books on sexual behavior and sexual functioning (e.g., *Sex for Dummies* by Westheimer).

13. Establish healthy and satisfying sexual relationships. (30, 31)

30. Assist the client in understanding the difference between healthy and potentially abusive or demeaning sexual relationships.

31. Encourage and support the client in her effort to become involved in a healthy sexual relationship.

14. Communicate constructively with partner about sexuality. (32, 33)

32. Role-play with the client healthy and effective communication about sexual thoughts, feelings, and desires.

33. Foster effective communication between the client and her partner about sexual preferences; provide feedback to the partners about their communication styles.

15. Engage in sensate focus activity alone and with partner to help

34. Assign the client body exploration and awareness

reduce anxiety and increase feelings of intimacy. (34, 35)

exercises (see *Sexual Awareness* by McCarthy and McCarthy).

35. Assign the client graduated steps of sexual pleasuring exercises with partner (see "Journaling the Response to Nondemand, Sexual Pleasuring [Sensate Focus]" in the *Adult Psychotherapy Homework Planner,* 2nd ed. by Jongsma).

16. Celebrate one's sexual and relational success. (36)

36. Validate the client's progress by identifying her strengths.

—. _____   —. _____

_____   _____

—. _____   —. _____

_____   _____

—. _____   —. _____

_____   _____

DIAGNOSTIC SUGGESTIONS:

Axis I:

302.71	Hypoactive Sexual Desire Disorder
302.79	Sexual Aversion Disorder
302.72	Female Sexual Arousal Disorder
302.73	Female Orgasmic Disorder
302.76	Dyspareunia
306.51	Vaginismus
302.70	Sexual Dysfunction NOS

_____   _____

_____   _____

Axis II:

V71.09	No Diagnosis
799.9	Diagnosis Deferred

_____   _____

_____   _____

SINGLE PARENTING

BEHAVIORAL DEFINITIONS

1. Experiences stress and fatigue associated with multiple roles and responsibilities.
2. Lacks financial and emotional support from child(ren)'s other parent
3. Fails to implement appropriate discipline and establish boundaries. ·
4. Verbalizes shame regarding single mother status and anxiety regarding prospects for mate.
5. Verbalizes guilt regarding child(ren)'s lack of an additional parent/rol model.   e
6. Experiences stress and anxiety regarding financial status and prospec for employment/career development   ts
7. Experiences conflicts in negotiating and managing visits and co-parenting with ex-spouse/partner.

—. _____
   _____
—. _____
   _____
—. _____
   _____

LONG-TERM GOALS

1. More effectively balance work, childcare/rearing, home, and other responsibilities.
2. Successfully negotiate financial, emotional, and physical demands of single parenting.
3. Develop a support system to assist in coping with stressors of single parenting.

4. Implement self-care strategies to maintain physical and emotional health.
5. Develop effective parenting strategies.

—. _____

    _____

—. _____

    _____

—. _____

    _____

SHORT-TERM OBJECTIVES

1. Describe the challenges, demands, and stressors associated with single parenting. (1, 2, 3)

2. Mourn the losses resulting from the end of a marriage/relationship and reduced economic resources. (4)

3. Explore values and socio-cultural influences related to single motherhood including associated stigma. (5)

THERAPEUTIC INTERVENTIONS

1. Develop and nurture a safe and trusting therapeutic relationship with the client; create a space for supportive sharing.

2. Validate the client's experiences of frustration, despair, and anxiety associated with single parenting and associated multiple roles.

3. Educate the client about the relationship between financial strain, chronic stress, poor psychological and physical health, and their influence on parenting.

4. Help the client identify losses and feelings related to the end of a marriage/relationship.

5. Explore with the client sociocultural influences on her attitudes and values associated with single mother status; assess the degree to which the client has

4. Identify and challenge internalized negative stereotypes of mother-headed households as deviant or deficient. (6, 7)

internalized these disparaging influences and its effects.

6. Explore the degree to which the client has internalized negative stereotypes about mother-headed households; assess the degree to which she has adopted feelings of shame and guilt regarding single mother status.

7. Challenge the client's internalized stereotypes and teach her to replace the notion of mother-headed households as deviant with the notion that it represents one variant within a range of many possible family configurations; affirm as normative the life experience of living in a one-parent family unit.

5. Identify and challenge unrealistic expectations regarding parenting. (8)

8. Help the client to identify and challenge unrealistic expectations about parenting (e.g., "Conflicts with my child are to be avoided at all costs"; "Parent-child conflicts are a sign that I am an ineffective parent").

6. Identify feelings and behavior related to attempting to balance work and family roles. (9)

9. Explore and identify the client's feelings of guilt, shame, and anxiety associated with not meeting internal or external expectations associated with balancing work and family roles.

7. Identify at least two internalized expectations and standards regarding multiple roles that are healthy and those that are potentially harmful; discard those that are harmful. (10)

10. Assist the client with identifying those expectations that are helpful and those that are potentially harmful; help the client discard those that are causing undue stress and strain (e.g., "I must balance all of my responsibilities smoothly and perfectly") and replace them with more realistic messages (e.g., "I will balance

8. Implement time management skills to more effectively balance multiple demands. (11, 12, 13)

my roles to the best of my ability, knowing that mistakes will be made").

11. Explore with the client strategies for making her life more manageable and less stressful.

12. Teach the client time management and simplification of household tasks (e.g., reducing ironing of wearing apparel to a minimum).

13. Assist the client in reframing simplification of tasks as timesaving changes as opposed to sloppy housekeeping.

9. Develop planning and problem-solving skills to more effectively cope with multiple demands. (14)

14. Role-play with the client planning and assertive problem-solving skills (e.g., planning and defining the needs for assistance; determining when help is needed, how to ask for help, and whom to ask).

10. Network with other single parents. (15)

15. Refer the client to a support group for single mothers.

11. Mobilize at least one ally who can serve as confidant and model for effective coping. (16)

16. Encourage the client to locate an ally who can serve as a source of support and a role model; review and process potential candidates.

12. Interact with a social support network for empathy, mutual aid, and ventilation of unresolved feelings and conflicts. (17, 18)

17. Facilitate the client's development of a social support network to assist with multiple roles and responsibilities.

18. Teach the client to effectively utilize external sources of support from family, friends, and other parents.

13. Recognize one's strengths and competencies. (19, 20)

19. Help the client to identify personal strengths that have enabled her to manage single parenting and can be applied in many situations and contexts.

14. Explore and obtain the education or training necessary to participate in the workforce or achieve job advancement. (21, 22)

15. Identify and implement stress management and self-care strategies. (23)

16. Challenge unrealistic attitudes regarding parenting and replace with more rational/realistic ones. (24)

17. Verbalize an understanding of the impact of a parent's reaction on a child's behavior. (25, 26)

20. Encourage the client to create her own affirmations and write them down.

21. Refer the client to appropriate educational and job training.

22. Role-play with the client job/career advancement strategies (e.g., negotiating skills).

23. Encourage the client to employ stress management and self-care activities (e.g., yoga, guided relaxation, exercise, massage, bubble baths).

24. Assess the degree to which the client has adopted unrealistic attitudes regarding parenting (e.g., "I am a bad mother if I spend time taking care of myself"); challenge the client's unrealistic attitudes and assist with replacing these with constructive thoughts.

25. Use a Parent Management Training approach beginning with teaching the client how parent and child behavioral interactions can encourage or discourage positive or negative behavior and how changing key elements of those interactions (e.g., prompting and reinforcing positive behaviors) can be used to promote positive change (e.g., *Parenting the Strong-Willed Child* by Forehand and Long).

26. Teach the client how to specifically define and identify problem behaviors; identify her reactions to the behavior, and determine whether the reaction encourages or discourages the

behavior; generate alternative constructive reactive behaviors.

18. Implement effective parenting practices/skills. (27, 28, 29)

27. Teach the client how to implement key parenting practices consistently, including establishing realistic age-appropriate rules for acceptable and unacceptable behavior, prompting of positive behavior in the environment, use of positive reinforcement to encourage behavior (e.g., praise), use of clear direct instruction, time out, and other loss-of-privilege practices for problem behavior, negotiation, and renegotiation (usually with older children and adolescents).

28. Assign the client home exercises in which she implements and records results of the implementation exercises; review in session, providing corrective feedback toward improved, appropriate, and consistent use of skills.

29. Role-play with the client effective parenting techniques; refer the client to books and videos on effective parenting (e.g., *1-2-3 Magic: Training Your Preschoolers and Preteens to Do What You Want* by Phelan; *Parenting with Love and Logic* by Cline and Fay; *Parenting Through Change* by Forgatch; *The Incredible Years* by Webster-Stratton).

19. Delegate responsibilities in the home. (30)

30. Help the client to allocate responsibilities of the home and promote wider distribution of household tasks with older children to keep the parental

system from being overloaded and achieve a more efficient use of time.

20. Reestablish or reorganize family rituals such as birthday celebrations and holidays. (31)

31. Help the client to reestablish or restructure family rituals (e.g., celebrations) in order to facilitate adaptation to a change in family structure.

21. Regularly schedule family sessions to assure a relatively smooth process of day-to-day activities. (32)

32. Discuss with the client ways of structuring and managing regular family meetings to ensure a relatively smooth process of daily activities, facilitate a more efficient use of time, and provide an opportunity for feedback and troubleshooting.

22. Describe the challenges of negotiating with the noncustodial parent. (33)

33. Validate the client's challenges and frustrations related to interacting with the noncustodial parent.

23. Implement at least two strategies to negotiate with noncustodial parent with limited to no conflict. (34, 35, 36)

34. Explore, along with the client, ways to interact with the noncustodial parent in order to minimize conflict and stress; help her to develop bargaining and conflict-resolution skills.

35. If feasible, refer the client and noncustodial parent to co-parenting counseling (not recommended in cases of family violence or in the case of a noncustodial parent with Antisocial or Narcissistic Personality Disorder).

36. Refer the client to legal and court resources related to enforcement of child support payments.

24. Increase or maintain socialization with other adults. (37)

37. Encourage the client to socialize with other adults to reduce feelings of vulnerability, depression, and disempowerment.

25. Identify the joys of single parenting. (38)

38. Assist the client with identifying and appreciating the positive aspects of parenting.

26. Verbalize increased feelings of self-esteem and self-empowerment. (39)

39. Help the client continue to pursue methods of feeling strong and supported (e.g., engage in personally meaningful and satisfying activities, maintain a support group and a healthy lifestyle).

—. _____   —. _____
   _____   _____
—. _____   —. _____
   _____   _____
—. _____   —. _____
   _____   _____

DIAGNOSTIC SUGGESTIONS:

Axis I:	309.0	Adjustment Disorder with Depressed Mood
	309.24	Adjustment Disorder with Anxiety
	309.28	Adjustment Disorder with Mixed Anxiety and Depressed Mood
	V61.10	Partner Relational Problem
	V61.20	Parent-Child Relational Problem
	V62.89	Phase of Life Problem
	_____	_____
	_____	_____
Axis II:	V71.09	No Diagnosis
	799.9	Diagnosis Deferred
	_____	_____
	_____	_____

Appendix A

BIBLIOTHERAPY

Anxiety

Bourne, E. J. (2005). *The Anxiety and Phobia Workbook,* 4th ed. Oakland, CA: New Harbinger Publications.

Burns, D. D. (2006). *When Panic Attacks: The New, Drug-free Anxiety Therapy That Can Change Your Life.* New York: Random House.

Hanan, J. (1999). *Coping with Changing Gender Roles.* Center City, MN: Hazelden Publishing.

Kennerley, H. (1997). *Overcoming Anxiety: A Self-Help Guide Using Cognitive Behavioral Techniques.* New York: NYU Press.

Lipman-Blumen, J. (1984). *Gender Roles and Power.* Upper Saddle River, NJ: Prentice-Hall.

Nolen-Hoeksema, S. (2003). *Women Who Think Too Much: How to Break Free.* New York: Henry Holt & Co.

Peurifoy, R. Z. (2005). *Anxiety, Phobias, and Panic: A Step-by-Step Program for Regaining Control of Your Life.* New York: Time-Warner.

Stetson, D. (2004). *Women's Rights in the U.S.A.: Policy Debates and Gender Roles.* New York: Taylor & Francis.

Balancing Work and Family/Multiple Roles

Bernstein, D. A., and Borkovec, T. D. (1973). *Progressive Relaxation Training.* Champaign, IL: Research Press.

Holtzworth-Munroe, A. S., and Jacobson, N. S. (1991). Behavioral marital therapy. In A. S. Gurman and D. P. Knickerson (Eds.), *Handbook of Family Therapy,* 2nd ed. (pp. 96–133). Levittown, PA: Brunner/Mazel.

Iovine, V. (2001). *The Girlfriends' Guide to Getting Your Groove Back: Loving Your Family without Losing Your Mind.* New York: Penguin.

Leith, L. (1998). *Exercising Your Way to Better Mental Health*. New York: Fitness Info Tech.

Rygh, J., and Sanderson, W. C. (2004). *Treating GAD: Evidence-Based Strategies, Tools, and Techniques*. New York: Guilford Press.

Zinbarg, R. E., Craske, M. G., Barlow, D. H., and O'Leary, T. (1993). *Mastery of Your Anxiety and Worry–Client Guide*. San Antonio, TX: The Psychological Corporation.

Body Image Disturbance/Eating Disorders

Boston Women's Health Book Collective (1998). *Our Bodies, Ourselves–For the New Century*. New York: Touchstone.

Cash, T. F. (1997). *The Body Image Workbook: An 8-Step Program for Learning to Like Your Looks*. Oakland, CA: New Harbinger Publications.

National Institute of Mental Health (2001). *Eating Disorders: Facts about Eating Disorders and the Search for Solutions* (NIH Publication No. 01-4901). Washington, D.C.: U.S. Government Printing Office.

Siegel, M., Brisman, J., and Weinshel, M. (1989). *Surviving an Eating Disorder: Strategies for Families and Friends*. New York: HarperCollins.

Wolf, N. (2002). *The Beauty Myth: How Images of Beauty Are Used Against Women*. New York: William Morrow.

Career Success Obstacles

Brooks, D., and Brooks, L. (2001). *Seven Secrets of Successful Women: Strategies of the Women Who've Made It*. New York: Fine Communications.

Daniels, J. T. (2002). *Power Tools for Women: Plugging into the Essential Skills for Work and Life*. New York: Crown Publishing.

Doyle, M. K. (2000). *Mentoring Heroes: 52 Fabulous Women's Paths to Success and the Mentors Who Empowered Them*. Batavia, IL: 3E Press.

Caregiving of Aging Parents

Beck, A. T., Rush, A. J., Shaw, B. F., and Emergy, G. (1979). *Cognitive Therapy of Depression*. New York: Guilford Press.

Jacobs, B. J. (2006). *The Emotional Survival Guide for Caregivers*. New York: Guilford Press.

Kuba, C. A. (2006). *Navigating the Journey of Aging Parents*. New York: Routledge.

Kübler-Ross, E., and Kessler, D. (2005). *On Grief and Grieving*. New York: Scribner.

Morris, V. (2004). *How to Care for Aging Parents*. New York: Workman Publishers.

Rhodes, L. (2005). *Caregiving as Your Parents Age: The Complete Guide to Helping Your Parents Age Gracefully, Happily, and Healthfully.* New York: Penguin.

Chemical Dependence

Jersilk, D. (2001). *Happy Hours: Alcohol in a Woman's Life.* New York: HarperCollins.
Miller, N. (2005). *The Fight Within: A Story of Women in Recovery.* Lincoln, NE: Ballantine.

Childbearing/Rearing Decisions

Davis, L., and Keyser, J. (1997). *Becoming the Parent You Want to Be: A Sourcebook of Strategies for the First Five Years.* New York: Broadway Books.
Eisenberg, A., Murkoff, H. E., and Hathaway, S. E. (1996). *What to Expect When You Are Expecting.* New York: Workman.
Eldridge, S. (1999). *Twenty Things Adopted Kids Wish Their Adoptive Parents Knew.* New York: Random House.
Iovine, V. (1995). *The Girlfriends' Guide to Pregnancy.* New York: Simon & Schuster.

Depression

Beck, A. T., Rush, A. J., Shaw, B. F., and Emergy, G. (1979). *Cognitive Therapy of Depression.* New York: Guilford Press.
Burns, D. D. (1999). *Feeling Good: The New Mood Therapy.* New York: William Morrow.
Jack, D. C. (1993). *Silencing the Self: Women and Depression.* New York: Harper.
Rosenthal, M. S. (2000). *Women and Depression.* New York: McGraw-Hill.
Sanders, D. (1989). *Women and Depression: A Practical Self-Help Guide.* London: SPCK Publishers.

Divorce

Bryan, P. E. (2006). *Constructive Divorce: Procedural Justice and Sociolegal Reform.* Washington, DC: American Psychological Association.
Colgrove, B., Bloomfield, D., and McWilliams, C. (1997). *How to Survive the Loss of a Love.* New York: Dolphin Books.
Forehand, R., and Long, N. (2002). *Parenting the Strong-Willed Child.* New York: McGraw-Hill.
Forgatch, M. (1994). *Parenting Through Change: A Training Manual.* Eugene, OR: Oregon Social Learning Center.

Neuman, M. G. (1998). *Helping Your Kids Cope with Divorce the Sandcastle Way.* New York: Random House.

Smith, G. R., and Abrahms, S. (1998). *What Every Woman Should Know About Divorce and Custody.* New York: Penguin.

Trimberger, E. K. (2005). *The New Single Woman.* Boston, MA: Beacon.

www.womansdivorce.com. Retrieved September 25, 2006.

Domestic Violence/Battery

Burns, D. (1993). *Ten Days to Self-Esteem!* New York: William Morrow.

Carthy, G. N., and Davidson, S. (2006). *You Can Be Free: An Easy-to-Read Handbook for Abused Women.* Emeryville, CA: Seal Press.

Kubany, E. S., McCaig, M. A., and Laconsay, J. R. (2003). *Healing the Trauma of Domestic Violence.* Oakland, CA: New Harbinger Publications.

Murphy-Milano, S. (2004). *Moving Out, Moving On: When a Relationship Goes Wrong Workbook.* Janesville, WI: Kindling Publishing.

Norwood, R. (1985). *Women Who Love Too Much.* New York: Simon & Schuster.

Norwood, R. (1997). Daily Meditations for Women Who Love Too Much. New York: Putnam.

Infertility

Daniluk, J. C. (2001). *The Infertility Survival Guide: Everything You Need to Know to Cope with the Challenges While Maintaining Your Sanity, Dignity and Relationships.* Oakland, CA: New Harbinger Publications.

Domar, A. D., and Kelly, A. L. (2004). *Conquering Infertility: Dr. Alice Domar's Mind/Body Guide to Enhancing Fertility and Coping with Infertility.* New York: Penguin Books.

Glazer, E. S. (1998). *The Long-Awaited Stork: A Guide to Parenting After Infertility.* San Francisco, CA: Jossey-Bass.

Gordon, E. (1992). *Mommy, Did I Grow in Your Tummy? Where Babies Come From.* Santa Monica, CA: EM Greenberg Press.

Johnston, P. R. (1994). *Adopting After Infertility.* Indianapolis, IN: Perspectives Press.

Peoples, D., and Rovner-Ferguson, H. (2000). *Experiencing Infertility: An Essential Resource.* New York: W. W. Norton & Company.

www.theafa.org, Retrieved September 25, 2006.

www.asrm.org. Retrieved September 25, 2006.

www.resolve.org. Retrieved September 25, 2006.

Low Self-Esteem/Lack of Assertiveness

Alberti, R. E., and Emmons, M. E. (Eds.) (2001). *Your Perfect Right: Assertiveness and Equality in Your Life and Relationships,* 8th ed. Atascadero, CA: Impact.

Braiker, H. B. (2001). *The Disease to Please: Curing the People-Pleasing Syndrome.* New York: McGraw-Hill.

Burns, D. (1993). *Ten Days to Self-Esteem!* New York: William Morrow.

McKay, M., and Fanning, P. (2001). *Self-Esteem,* 3rd ed. Oakland, CA: New Harbinger Publications.

Schiraldi, G. R. (2001). *The Self-Esteem Workbook.* Oakland, CA: New Harbinger Publications.

Menopause and Perimenopause

Goldman, C. (Ed.) (2004). *The Ageless Spirit: Reflections on Living Life to the Fullest in Midlife and the Years Beyond,* 2nd ed. Minneapolis, MN: Fairview.

Northrup, C. (2004). *The Wisdom of Menopause.* New York: Random House.

Somers, S. (2004). *The Sexy Years.* New York: Random House.

www.healthywomen.org. Retrieved September 25, 2006.

Partner Relational Problems

Bach, G., and Wyden, P. (1976). *The Intimate Enemy: How to Fight Fair in Love and Marriage.* New York: Avon Books.

Burns, J. (2006). *Creating an Intimate Marriage.* Minneapolis, MN: Bethany House.

Colgrove, M., Bloomfield, H., and McWilliams, P. (1991). *How to Survive the Loss of a Love.* Los Angeles: Prelude Press.

Forward, S. (1991). *Obsessive Love: When It Hurts Too Much to Let Go.* New York: Bantam.

Hendrix, H. (1988). *Getting the Love You Want.* New York: Henry Holt.

Holtzworth-Munroe, A. S., and Jacobson, N. S. (1991). Behavioral marital therapy. In A. S. Gurman and D. P. Knickerson (Eds.), *Handbook of Family Therapy,* 2nd ed. (pp. 96–133). Levittown, PA: Brunner/Mazel.

Murphy-Milano, S. (2004). *Moving Out, Moving On: When a Relationship Goes Wrong Workbook.* Janesville, WI: Kindling Publishing.

Oberlin, L. (2005). *Surviving Separation and Divorce: A Woman's Guide.* Avon, MA: Adams Media.

Postpartum Mood Disorders (PPD)

Dunnewold, A., and Sanford, D. G. (1994). *Postpartum Survival Guide*. Oakland, CA: New Harbinger Publications.

Kendall-Tackett, K. A. (2005). *Depression in New Mothers: Causes, Consequences, and Treatment Alternatives*. New York: Haworth.

Kleiman, K. R., and Raskin, V. D. (1994). *This Isn't What I Expected: Overcoming* Postpartum Depression. New York: Bantam.

Postpartum Support International. www.postpartum.net/brief/html.

Weissbluth, M. (1999). *Healthy Sleep Habits, Happy Child*. New York: Ballantine.

www.postpartum.net. Retrieved September 25, 2006.

Sexual Abuse (Childhood)

Bass, E. and Davis, L. (1994). *The Courage to Heal: A Guide for Women Survivors of Child Sexual Abuse,* 3rd ed. New York: HarperCollins.

Cloud, H., and Townsend, J. (1995). *Safe People: How to Find Relationships That Are Good for You and Avoid Those That Aren't*. Grand Rapids, MI: Zondervan.

Courtois, C. A. (1996). *Healing the Incest Wound: Adult Survivors in Therapy*. New York: Norton.

Katherine, A. (1991). *Boundaries: Where You End and I Begin*. New York: Fireside Publications.

Maltz, W. (2001). *The Sexual Healing Journey: A Guide for Survivors of Sexual Abuse*. New York: HarperCollins.

Sexual Assault and Rape

Cloud, H., and Townsend, J. (1999). *Boundaries in Marriage*. Grand Rapids, MI: Zondervan.

Cloud, H., and Townsend, J. (2000). *Boundaries in Dating: Making Dating Work*. Grand Rapids, MI: Zondervan.

Katherine, A. (1991). *Boundaries: Where You End and I Begin*. New York: Fireside Publications.

Maltz, W. (2001). *The Sexual Healing Journey: A Guide for Survivors of Sexual Abuse*. New York: HarperCollins.

Matsakis, A. (2003). *The Rape Recovery Handbook: Step-by-Step Help for Survivors of Sexual Assault*. Oakland, CA: New Harbinger Publications.

Sexuality/Issues in Sexual Functioning

Alan Guttmacher Institute. http://www.guttmacher.org. Retrieved May 7, 2006.

Barbach, L. (2000). *For Yourself: The Fulfillment of Female Sexuality.* New York: Signet.

Copeland, M. E., and Harris, M. (2000). *Healing the Trauma of Abuse: A Woman's Workbook.* Oakland, CA: New Harbinger Publications.

Dodson, B. (1987). *Sex for One: The Joy of Self-loving*, New York: Harmony Books.

McCarthy, B., and McCarthy, E. (1984). *Sexual Awareness.* New York: Carroll & Graf.

Planned Parenthood (n.d.). *Women's Health: Sexuality.* Http://www.plannedparenthood .org/pp2/portal/medicalinfo/femalesexualhealth/. Retrieved May 7, 2006.

Sexuality Information and Education Council of the United States. http://siecus.org. Retrieved May 7, 2006.

Sinclair Intimacy Institute. *Better Sex Video Series: Volumes 1–3.*

Tiefer, L. (2001). A new view of women's sexual problems: Why new? Why now? *Journal of Sex Research, 38,* 89–96.

Westheimer, R. (1995). *Sex for Dummies.* New York: IDG Books.

Single Parenting

Cline, F., and Fay, J. (1990). *Parenting with Love and Logic.* Colorado Springs, CO: NavPress.

Ellison, S. (2000). *The Courage to Be a Single Mother: Becoming Whole Again After Divorce.* New York: HarperCollins.

Forehand, R., and Long, N. (2002). *Parenting the Strong-Willed Child.* New York: McGraw-Hill.

Forgatch, M. (1994). *Parenting Through Change: A Training Manual.* Eugene, OR: Oregon Social Learning Center.

Howard, J. (1998). *Bringing Up Boys: A Parenting Manual for Sole Mothers Raising Sons.* Melbourne, Australia: The Australia Council for Educational Research.

Nelson, J., Erwin, C., and Delzer, C. (1994). *Positive Discipline for Single Parents: A Practical Guide to Raising Children Who Are Responsible, Respectful, and Resourceful.* Rocklin, CA: Prima.

Phelan, T. (1995). *1-2-3 Magic: Training Your Preschoolers and Preteens to Do What You Want.* Glen Ellyn, IL: Child Management, Inc.

Webster-Stratton, C. (1992). *The Incredible Years.* Toronto, Canada: Umbrella Press.

Appendix B

BIBLIOGRAPHY OF PROFESSIONAL REFERENCES

American Psychological Association (2006). *Guidelines for Psychological Practice with Girls and Women.* Manuscript submitted for publication.

Ancis, J. R. (Ed.) (2004). *Culturally Responsive Interventions: Innovative Approaches to Working with Diverse Populations.* New York: Brunner-Routledge.

Ballou, M., and Brown, L. (Eds.) (2002). *Rethinking Mental Health and Disorder: Feminist Perspectives.* New York: Guilford Press.

Beck, A. T., Rush, A. J., Shaw, B. F., and Emergy, G. (1979). *Cognitive Therapy of Depression.* New York: Guilford Press.

Bernstein, D. A., and Borkovec, T. D. (1973). *Progressive Relaxation Training.* Champaign, IL: Research Press.

Bryan, P. E. (2006). *Constructive Divorce: Procedural Justice and Sociolegal Reform.* Washington, DC: American Psychological Association.

Comas-Díaz, L., and Greene, B. (Eds.) (1994). *Women of Color: Integrating Ethnic and Gender Identities in Psychotherapy.* New York: Guilford Press.

Fallon, F. (1994). *Feminist Perspectives on Eating Disorders.* New York: Guilford Press.

Fassinger, R. E. (1996). Hitting the ceiling: Gendered barriers to occupational entry, advancement, and achievement. In L. Diamant and J. Lee (Eds.), *The Psychology of Sex, Gender, and Jobs: Issues and Solutions* (pp. 21–46). Westport, CT: Greenwood.

Finkelhor, D. (1990). Early and long-term effects of childhood sexual abuse: An update. *Professional Psychology: Research and Practice, 21,* 325–330.

Fitzgerald, L. F., and Nutt, R. (1986). The Division 17 principles concerning the counseling/psychotherapy of women: Rationale and implementation. *The Counseling Psychologist, 14,* 180–216.

Gerrity, D. A. (2001). Five medical treatment stages of infertility: Implications for counselors. *Family Journal: Counseling and Therapy for Couples and Families, 9,* 140–150.

Herman, J. (1992). *Trauma and Recovery.* New York: Basic Books.

Holtzworth-Munroe, A. S., and Jacobson, N. S. (1991). Behavioral marital therapy. In A. S. Gurman and D. P. Knickerson (Eds.), *Handbook of Family Therapy,* 2nd ed. (pp. 96–133). Levittown, PA: Brunner/Mazel.

Jackson, L. C., and Greene, B. (Eds.) (2000). *Psychotherapy with African-American Women.* New York: Guilford Press.

Jongsma, A. E. (2006). *Adult Psychotherapy Homework Planner,* 2nd ed. New York: John Wiley & Sons.

Kendall-Tackett, K. A. (2005). *Depression in New Mothers: Causes, Consequences, and Treatment Alternatives.* New York: Haworth.

Maass, S. V., and Neely, M. A. (2000). *Counseling Single Parents: A Cognitive-Behavioral Approach.* New York: Springer.

Milgrom, J., Martin, P. R., and Negri, L. M. (1999). *Treating Postnatal Depression: A Psychological Approach for Health Care Practitioners.* New York: John Wiley & Sons.

National Center on Addiction and Substance Abuse (2005). *Women Under the Influence.* Baltimore, MD: Johns Hopkins University Press.

National Institute of Mental Health (2001). *Eating Disorders: Facts about Eating Disorders and the Search for Solutions* (NIH Publication No. 01-4901). Washington, DC: U.S. Government Printing Office.

Rygh, J., and Sanderson, W. C. (2004*). Treating GAD: Evidence-Based Strategies, Tools, and Techniques.* New York: Guilford Press.

Taylor, V. (1996). *Rock-a-by Baby: Feminism, Self-Help, and Postpartum Depression.* New York: Routledge.

Tiefer, L. (2001). A new view of women's sexual problems: Why new? Why now? *Journal of Sex Research, 38,* 89–96.

Unger, R. (Ed.) (2001). *Handbook of the Psychology of Women and Gender.* New York: John Wiley & Sons.

Walker, L. E. A. (1994). *Abused Women and Survivor Therapy.* Washington, DC: American Psychological Association.

Weissbluth, M. (1999). *Healthy Sleep Habits, Happy Child.* New York: Ballantine.

Worell, J. (Ed.) (2001). *Encyclopedia of Women and Gender: Sex Similarities and Differences and the Impact of Society on Gender (Vol. 1 and 2).* San Diego, CA: Academic Press.

Appendix C

INDEX OF *DSM-IV-TR* CODES ASSOCIATED WITH PRESENTING PROBLEMS

Acute Stress Disorder   308.3
Anxiety
Caregiving of Aging Parents
Sexual Assault and Rape

Adjustment Disorder with Anxiety   309.24
Anxiety
Balancing Work and Family/Multiple Roles
Career Success Obstacles
Caregiving of Aging Parents
Childbearing/Rearing Decisions
Divorce
Partner Relational Problems
Sexual Assault and Rape
Single Parenting

Adjustment Disorder with Depressed Mood   309.0
Balancing Work and Family/Multiple Roles
Career Success Obstacles
Caregiving of Aging Parents
Childbearing/Rearing Decisions
Depression
Divorce
Infertility
Partner Relational Problems
Sexual Assault and Rape
Single Parenting

Adjustment Disorder with Mixed Anxiety and Depressed Mood   309.28
Balancing Work and Family/Multiple Roles
Career Success Obstacles
Caregiving of Aging Parents
Childbearing/Rearing Decisions
Divorce
Infertility
Menopause and Perimenopause
Single Parenting

Alcohol Abuse   305.00
Chemical Dependence

Alcohol Dependence   303.90
Chemical Dependence
Domestic Violence/Battery
Sexual Abuse (Childhood)
Sexual Assault and Rape

Amphetamine Abuse   305.70
Chemical Dependence

Amphetamine Dependence   304.40
Chemical Dependence

Anorexia Nervosa   307.1
Body Image Disturbance/Eating Disorders

Anxiety Disorder Not Otherwise Specified 300.00
Anxiety
Career Success Obstacles

Avoidant Personality Disorder 301.82
Domestic Violence/Battery
Low Self-Esteem/Lack of Assertiveness
Sexual Abuse (Childhood)
Sexual Assault and Rape

Bereavement V62.82
Caregiving of Aging Parents
Depression

Bipolar I Disorder 296.xx
Depression
Postpartum Mood Disorders (PPD)

Bipolar II Disorder 296.89
Depression
Postpartum Mood Disorders (PPD)

Borderline Personality Disorder 301.83
Domestic Violence/Battery
Sexual Abuse (Childhood)
Sexual Assault and Rape

Breathing-Related Sleep Disorder 780.59
Menopause and Perimenopause

Brief Psychotic Disorder 298.8
Postpartum Mood Disorders (PPD)

Bulimia Nervosa 307.51
Body Image Disturbance/Eating Disorders

Cannabis Dependence 304.30
Chemical Dependence

Cocaine Abuse 305.60
Chemical Dependence

Cocaine Dependence 304.20
Chemical Dependence

Cyclothymic Disorder 301.13
Depression

Dependent Personality Disorder 301.6
Divorce
Domestic Violence/Battery
Low Self-Esteem/Lack of Assertiveness
Sexual Abuse (Childhood)
Sexual Assault and Rape

Depressive Disorder Not Otherwise Specified 311
Depression
Sexual Assault and Rape

Dissociative Identity Disorder 300.14
Domestic Violence/Battery
Sexual Abuse (Childhood)
Sexual Assault and Rape

Dyspareunia (Not Due to a General Medical Condition) 302.76
Sexuality/Issues in Sexual Functioning

Dysthymic Disorder 300.4
Balancing Work and Family/Multiple Roles
Childbearing/Rearing Decisions
Depression
Domestic Violence/Battery
Infertility
Low Self-Esteem/Lack of Assertiveness
Menopause and Perimenopause
Sexual Abuse (Childhood)
Sexual Assault and Rape

Eating Disorder Not Otherwise Specified 307.50
Body Image Disturbance/Eating Disorders

Physical Abuse of Adult (if focus of clinical attention is on victim) 995.81
Domestic Violence/Battery

Polysubstance Dependence 304.80
Chemical Dependence
Domestic Violence/Battery
Sexual Abuse (Childhood)
Sexual Assault and Rape

Posttraumatic Stress Disorder 309.81
Domestic Violence/Battery
Partner Relational Problems
Sexual Abuse (Childhood)
Sexual Assault and Rape

Primary Insomnia 307.42
Menopause and Perimenopause

Relational Problem Not Otherwise Specified V62.81
Depression

Relational Problem Related to... [*Indicate the General Medical Condition*] V61.9
Infertility
Menopause and Perimenopause

Schizoaffective Disorder 295.70
Depression

Sedative, Hypnotic, or Anxiolytic Dependence 304.10
Chemical Dependence

Separation Anxiety Disorder 309.21
Anxiety
Divorce

Sexual Abuse of Adult (if focus of clinical attention is on victim) 995.83
Sexual Abuse (Childhood)
Sexual Assault and Rape

Sexual Abuse of Child (if focus of clinical attention is on victim) 995.53
Sexual Abuse (Childhood)

Sexual Aversion Disorder 302.79
Sexuality/Issues in Sexual Functioning

Sexual Dysfunction Not Otherwise Specified 302.70
Sexuality/Issues in Sexual Functioning

Social Phobia 300.23
Anxiety
Low Self-Esteem/Lack of Assertiveness

Vaginismus (Not Due to a Medical Condition) 306.51
Sexuality/Issues in Sexual Functioning